Geography

ages 5–7

Stuart May, Paula Richardson & Emma Till

Published by Scholastic Ltd,
Villiers House,
Clarendon Avenue,
Leamington Spa,
Warwickshire
CV32 5PR
www.scholastic.co.uk

Printed by Bell & Bain Ltd, Glasgow
Text © 2002 Stuart May, Paula Richardson and Emma Till
© 2002 Scholastic Ltd
1 2 3 4 5 6 7 8 9 0   2 3 4 5 6 7 8 9 0 1

Authors
Stuart May, Paula Richardson and Emma Till

Editor
Roanne Davis

Assistant Editor
Dulcie Booth

Series designer
Lynne Joesbury

Designer
Paul Cheshire

Illustrations
Chantal Kees

Cover illustration
Jill Newton

British Library Cataloguing-in-Publication Data
A catalogue record for this book is available from the British Library.

ISBN 0-439-98311-8

Designed using Adobe Pagemaker

Contents

Acknowledgements

Andersen Press Ltd for the use of text and illustrations from *Dr Xargle's Book of Earth Weather* by Jeanne Willis. Text © 1992, Jeanne Willis; illustrations ©1992, Tony Ross (1992, Red Fox).

Cannon Hall Farm for the use of text and illustrations from Cannon Hall Farm publicity material © 2001, Cannon Hall Farm.

The Geographical Association and Worldaware for the use of text and adapted map from *Tocuaro – A Mexican Village: Pupil's Book KS2* by Vincent Bruce and Wendy Morgan © 1985, The Geographical Association and Worldaware (1998, Worldaware).

The Geographical Association for the use of text and illustrations from *Barnaby Bear to the Rescue* by Elaine Jackson © 2001, The Geographical Association; *Barnaby Bear Goes to Dublin* by Elaine Jackson © 2000, The Geographical Association; *Barnaby Bear Goes to Brittany* by Elaine Jackson © 2000, The Geographical Association. Illustrations by Roland Piper based on those by Roland Piper in the original books © 2002, Roland Piper. Barnaby Bear passport and photograph courtesy of TTS Ltd from the Barnaby Bear suitcase. Barnaby Bear is registered to The Geographical Association as a trademarked item.

HarperCollins Publishers for the use of an illustration from *The Day Veronica was Nosy* by Colin Reeder and Elizabeth Laird. Illustration © 1990, Colin Reeder and Elizabeth Laird (1990, HarperCollins Publishers).

Hodder and Stoughton Publishers for the use of an extract 'Bucket and spade' from *Local Ecology* by Kay Davies and Wendy Oldfield © 1992, Kay Davies and Wendy Oldfield (1992, Wayland Publishers); for the use of an extract 'Exploring the coastline' from *Starting Geography – Landscapes* by Helen Barden © 1992, Helen Barden (1992, Wayland Publishers).

Marian Lines for the use of 'Carbreakers' from *Tower Blocks* by Marian Lines © Marian Lines (Franklin Watts).

Longleat for the use of text from the Longleat publicity material © 2001, Longleat; for the use of the Longleat Estate Office map from Longleat publicity material (01985 844400) © 2001, Ballyhoo Publicity Ltd.

Mantra Publishers Ltd for the use of text and an illustration from *Packed Lunch for the Castle* by Steven Eales and Rachel and Chris Mendes. Text © 1987, Steven Eales; illustration © 1987, Rachel and Chris Mendes.

Penguin Books Ltd for the use of text and illustration from *Stanley Bagshaw and the 22 Ton Whale* by Bob Wilson © 1983, Bob Wilson (1983, Hamish Hamilton); for the use of text and illustration from *Blossom Comes Home* by James Herriot and Ruth Brown. Text © 1988, James Herriot; illustration ©1988, Ruth Brown (1988, Michael Joseph); for the use of an illustration from *Cops and Robbers* by Janet and Allan Ahlberg © 1999, Janet and Allan Ahlberg (1999, Puffin).

The Random House Group for the use of text and an illustration from *The Little House by the Sea* by Benedict Blathwayt © 1992, Benedict Blathwayt (1992, Julia MacRae); for the use of an illustration from *Bella's Big Adventure* by Benedict Blathwayt © 1996, Benedict Blathwayt (1996, Red Fox); for the use of text and illustration from *The Wind Blew* by Pat Hutchins © 1974, Pat Hutchins (1974, Bodley Head Children's Books).

Usborne Publishing for the use of text and illustrations from *Moving House* by Anne Civardi and Stephen Cartwright. Text © 1985, Anne Civardi; illustrations © 1985, Stephen Cartwright. Reproduced by permission of Usborne Publishing Ltd 83-85 Saffron Hill, London EC1N 8RT.

Walker Books Ltd for the use of text and illustrations from *When We Went to the Park* by Shirley Hughes © 1986, Shirley Hughes (1986, Walker Books); for the use of text and illustrations from *We're Going on a Bear Hunt* by Michael Rosen and Helen Oxenbury. Text © 1989, Michael Rosen; illustrations © 1989, Helen Oxenbury (1989, Walker Books).

Every effort has been made to trace copyright holders and the publishers apologise for any omissions.

Introduction

The texts selected for this book reflect the authors' belief that literacy entails not only reading and understanding texts and the ability to obtain information from a variety of sources, but also the ability to be selective and critical of the information gathered. As well as being selected for their geographical content, texts have been chosen to be interesting and informative; to offer a variety of formats and genres and to stimulate the children to find out more about the topic and to apply the skills and understanding gained directly from the activities associated with each text.

We have also interpreted the term 'text' liberally to include annotated maps and pictures, since pictures often carry a large amount of supplementary information that can be easily overlooked unless we make children aware of their potential.

There are many ways of using these texts to develop geographical learning. Even though they have been themed in chapters, many of them can be extracted and used to contribute to other themes within the geography curriculum.

Many of the texts tackle general themes, whilst others are more specific. It is important that you extend the more specific texts to set them within a more general context, and that the general texts are developed by reference to the more specific. In both cases, your own local area can provide what is needed, either to illustrate a general point by reference to a local example, or by making comparisons between your local area and more distant places or wider themes developed in the texts.

Teaching geography through texts

Texts are an essential component of geography, by its very nature. We cannot possibly study all of geography 'at firsthand' – the world is far too big for that. However much we develop the use of firsthand experience and fieldwork in our school geography, we will still gather most of our information from text in a variety of forms, for example labels or captions, notes, sentences, sustained writing.

Text will rarely, especially with young children, occur on its own; it will usually be combined with other ways of conveying information, such as pictures and photographs; diagrams; maps, pictorial or otherwise; timetables or other tabulated data.

Text can also reflect the type of society from which it comes, either in the form of the writing style or alphabet used, or as a story reflecting the traditions of that society.

Geographical enquiry

The texts included here are suitable to support geographical enquiry with young children. The children should be encouraged to ask questions about points raised in the texts, about the background from which it came or, for information texts, the processes and knowledge included. According to the specific text, it may be used as *information* or as a *stimulus* or, sometimes, both. Encourage the children to pose questions as a response to the texts – to find out more or to *question the text*. Try to get them to recognise that there some texts that will *answer* questions, while some will *pose* questions; some, of course, will do both if looked at critically, as the answers to some questions will generate more questions. This is how we all learn, by following a trail of questions and answers.

The National Literacy Strategy

These texts, although chosen for their geographical content, are designed to link to the National Literacy Strategy. They offer:

◆ a variety of genres
◆ extracts from stories – children should be encouraged to read the stories in full
◆ a range of vocabulary related to the subject
◆ word-, sentence- and text-level work
◆ opportunities for prediction and reflection
◆ opportunities to put into practice what has been learned
◆ opportunities for discussion, so developing speaking and listening skills as well as critical thinking.

Teaching with text and ICT

There are a variety of opportunities within this book to integrate ICT with the geography and literacy work undertaken. Use a selection of these to develop the use of ICT with your class:

◆ Writing stories, individually or co-operatively, over time or at one time
◆ Using drawing programs to make and label maps and diagrams
◆ Writing labels
◆ Making graphs and charts
◆ Writing descriptions comparing texts
◆ Reordering text
◆ Giving and following directions, for example using a map on screen or programming a floor turtle
◆ Sequencing text and producing a simple map from the sequenced text.

You will generate your own ideas for using the texts in this book as you get to know it more. The important thing to remember is that this book is designed to develop geographical knowledge, skills and understanding through the use of texts. The more children are able to use texts properly and critically, the better they will be able to learn in any subject, but the more they enjoy texts, the more they will want to learn. Never work on a text so much that it takes that enjoyment away. Let the story, especially, come through.

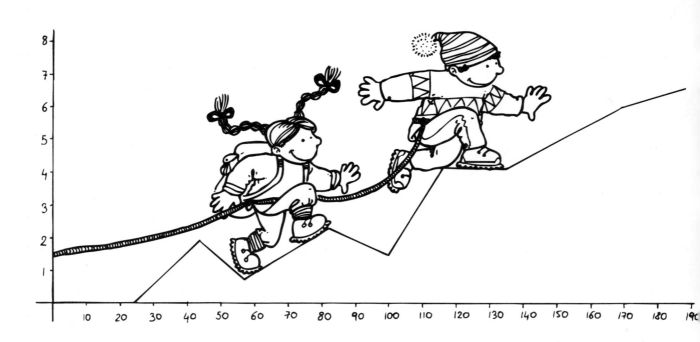

EXTRACT	GENRE	GEOGRAPHY LEARNING OBJECTIVES	LITERACY LEARNING OBJECTIVES	PAGE
When We Went to the Park	Narrative fiction	1c, 2a, 3a, 3c, 4b, 5a, 6a	◆ To make predictions from a text. ◆ To discuss character development. ◆ To draw and label items from a setting.	76
Shopping	Report with illustrations	3a, 3c, 3d, 4a, 6a	◆ To understand particular terms and phrases. ◆ To match text with pictures. ◆ To understand possessive apostrophes.	79
Cannon Hall Open Farm	Visitor's leaflet, advertisement	1c, 2c, 2e, 3c, 3e, 4a, 4b, 5a	◆ To extract information from a brochure. ◆ To recognise and use website and e-mail addresses. ◆ To identify persuasive words and phrases.	82
Our town	Labelled illustration	2a, 3a, 3d, 4b, 6a	◆ To read and write labels and captions. ◆ To use prepositions. ◆ To explore tenses.	87
Bella's Big Adventure	Story in a familiar setting	2a, 3d, 5a	◆ To use a story planner. ◆ To discuss points of view. ◆ To label a picture.	90
Gosling Farm	Labelled pictorial map	2c, 3a, 3d, 4a	◆ To read multisyllabic words. ◆ To investigate proper nouns. ◆ To create characters.	94
Town and country	Information text with diagrams	2a, 2c, 3c, 3d, 4b, 6b	◆ To predict words and phrases. ◆ To experiment with sentence meanings. ◆ To extract information.	97

Environmental geography

EXTRACT	GENRE	GEOGRAPHY LEARNING OBJECTIVES	LITERACY LEARNING OBJECTIVES	PAGE
Children who made a difference	Picture story in a familiar setting	3c, 5a, 5b	◆ To predict plots and outcomes. ◆ To sequence text and pictures. ◆ To write letters. ◆ To explore newspaper layout.	101
Our house, our street	Picture with labels and question/instruction captions	1b, 1c, 3c	◆ To develop the use of questions and instructions. ◆ To compare fiction and non-fiction. ◆ To practise punctuation.	104
Recycling questionnaire	Tick-chart questionnaire	3c, 5a, 5b	◆ To use and devise questionnaires. ◆ To read and create slogans. ◆ To investigate alliteration.	107
Carbreakers	Descriptive poem with rhythm and an ABCB rhyming pattern	1c, 3a, 3c, 5b	◆ To read poetry with expression. ◆ To revise contractions. ◆ To introduce metaphors.	110
Rules for the playground	Instructions/rules	1c, 2b, 2e, 4a, 5b	◆ To revise imperative verbs. ◆ To devise rules of conduct. ◆ To investigate positive and negative language.	113
The Country Code	Instructions/code of practice	2a, 2d, 3c, 3d, 5a, 5b	◆ To investigate sentence construction. ◆ To revise punctuation. ◆ To identify and use verbs.	116
Bucket and spade	Information with elements of argument	4a, 4b, 5a	◆ To identify non-fiction. ◆ To extract information and conduct further research. ◆ To discuss 'facts'.	119
We're Going on a Bear Hunt	Story with predictable and patterned language	2a, 2c, 3a, 3c, 4a	◆ To explore rhythm and pattern in text. ◆ To sequence events. ◆ To use vocabulary for sounds.	122

Geographical skills

EXTRACT	GENRE	GEOGRAPHY LEARNING OBJECTIVES	LITERACY LEARNING OBJECTIVES	PAGE
Longleat	Pictorial map with labels and captions – persuasive presentation	1c, 2c, 3a, 3b, 4a	◆ To use keys/legends. ◆ To revise proper nouns. ◆ To identify words and phrases typical of advertising.	126
Cops and Robbers	Story illustration including a labelled and annotated map	1d, 2a, 2c, 2e, 3a	◆ To retrieve information from lists and maps. ◆ To recognise street names. ◆ To use phonemes to group words.	130
Going to the country – part 1	Story in a familiar setting	2a, 2e, 3a, 3d, 4a	◆ To predict outcomes. ◆ To retell a story. ◆ To use contextual clues to understand certain vocabulary.	133
Going to the country – part 2	Story in a familiar setting	2e, 3a, 3d	◆ To recall a story. ◆ To use dialogue in role-play. ◆ To revise punctuation of dialogue.	136
Using an atlas	Contents and index pages of an atlas	2a, 2c, 3b, 3e	◆ To use contents and index pages. ◆ To practise alphabetical order. ◆ To find and write about facts that interest them.	139
Geographical dictionary	Explanation – illustrated dictionary definitions	2a, 2c, 2e, 3a, 4b	◆ To use a dictionary. ◆ To understand and use technical terms. ◆ To explore homographs.	142

Places

The awareness and understanding of places is fundamental to primary geography. Whilst very young children's geographical experience will be related mainly to their own locality, most will have had some experience of other places, either in the UK or elsewhere, by visiting relatives, going on holidays or day visits.

By the beginning of Key Stage 1, children will also have acquired some awareness of the wider world from television programmes and news items. However, all this knowledge will be partial – incomplete, unorganised and containing many misconceptions and probably stereotypes as well.

One of the most important objectives for primary geography is to allow children to develop a 'locational framework' where their knowledge of places can be put into a wider context and ensure that they develop a sense of 'belonging' as citizens of the wider world. Such a context will also allow them to relate their knowledge and understanding of one place (their own) to their knowledge and understanding of other places.

Studying specific places in depth encourages understanding of how and why people live differently in various parts of the world. Taught with sensitivity and awareness of issues, this will help to replace shallow stereotypes with real understanding.

This work continues throughout the primary stage. Key Stage 1 lays the foundations for both the locational framework and the more specific place studies. The longer Key Stage 2 allows more opportunity to study in depth and to consolidate and fill in details of the locational knowledge and understanding.

The texts in this chapter reflect these objectives by raising awareness of specific places (Tocuaro) and developing a general mental map of the world (the physical world map) as well as considering how we travel from place to place and why we sometimes move from one place to another.

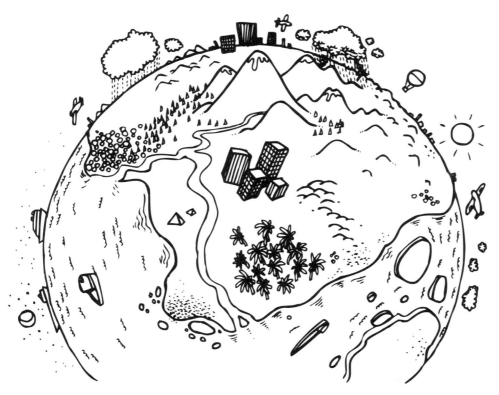

Physical world map

Genre
labelled map

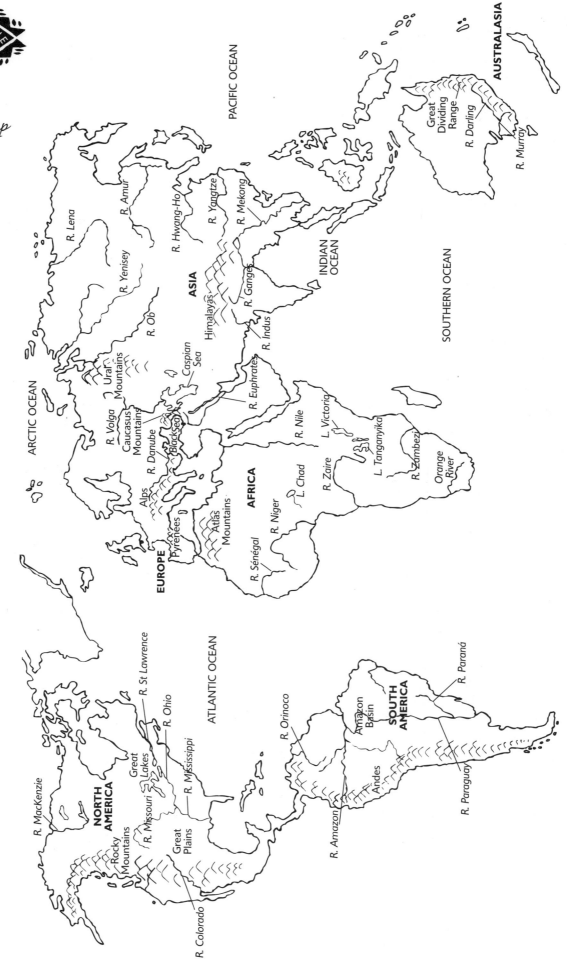

This map shows where the world's main mountain ranges, oceans, rivers and lakes are.

10

TEACHING WITH TEXT GEOGRAPHY ages 5–7

SCHOLASTIC

PLACES

Physical world map

Geography learning objectives

◆ To use geographical vocabulary (2a).

◆ To use maps to locate places on a worldwide scale (2c).

◆ To recognise physical and human features (3a).

◆ To identify and describe where places are (3b).

Background notes

This text can be used to help build up locational knowledge. It gives a simple and straightforward map of the physical features of the world, together with straightforward labels.

Vocabulary

Mountains, lakes, oceans, rivers, basin, range, plain, physical world, continent.

Discussing the text

◆ Before reading the text, take a general look at the map and examine its layout and the styles of text used. Why are some of the words in capitals? (For example, *PACIFIC OCEAN* – a major feature of the world.)

◆ What is the purpose of the text below the title? Why is this included? (To introduce the map and briefly explain what it shows.) Discuss the punctuation used in this section – particularly the commas that separate items in a list. Read the text to the children with and without the punctuation. What difference does it make?

◆ Point out the abbreviations in the labels, such as *R. Nile, L. Chad*. Do the children know that *R.* stands for *River* and *L.* for *Lake*? Can the children think of any abbreviations that we use every day? (For example, *PE, RE, TV*.)

◆ Look at some of the other names of places and features, helping the children to read the more difficult words. Demonstrate the use of capital letters for proper nouns.

◆ Discuss the advantages and disadvantages of labelling the map in this way. Are all the words easy to read? How else could you label the text? (For example, a key.)

◆ Talk about the labels on the map. What other maps have the children come across and how were they labelled? (For instance, a non-physical world map with the countries marked.) Explain that, in certain contexts, labels are essential for understanding and clarity.

◆ Discuss any unfamiliar words in the text and give simple explanations for the more difficult vocabulary, such as *mountain ranges* and *Amazon Basin*.

Geography activities

◆ Discuss with the children the differences between human and physical features. Which does this map show? How far does the map extend? What does it not show? (For example, it does not show either the North or South Poles. It is a *physical* map, and so the borders of the different countries are not shown.) Can the children find where Britain is? Make sure the children know what *continent* means and can relate the term to the land masses on the map, then covering the labels, ask them to identify the various continents shown.

◆ Create a word list of physical features such as *river, stream, lake, hill, marsh, mountain, valley, stream* and so on. Ask the children to help you sort them into two groups on a board or flip chart – water features and land features. Show some pictures of a variety of features and ask the children to identify each of them. Try to include examples from around the world.

◆ Help the children to identify the continents again on the map, and then ask them to list them according to different criteria, for example alphabetical or size. Compare this map with other world maps that show Antarctica. Is this a continent? (It is, because unlike the polar ice in the Arctic, there is a land mass under the ice.)

◆ Ask the children which continents certain features are in. Revisit any work the children have done on directions by asking them such questions as *Which continent is west of Europe?* or ... *east of South America?*

◆ Tell the children that Australasia is sometimes called Oceania. Look at the map together and decide why this might be a better name for it. Australasia/Oceania includes not only Australia but also New Zealand and many of the island groups to the east and some of those to the north.

◆ Use the map in tandem with a globe and ask the children to identify specific places on both. Why are both globes and maps used? Why is a map better to use in a book? (A globe is a truer representation of the Earth, showing the places in their correct relative shapes and sizes and relationships to each other; a flat map, on the other hand, *has* to be distorted to make it flat – but a map is far more convenient to put in a book, or to carry around with you!)

◆ Create a large floor map of the world or use a large floor puzzle of the world. Give out small cards with the names of seas, continents, countries and so on written on and ask groups of children to place them correctly on the floor map. Each group will need an atlas to refer to when there is uncertainty about the correct location. Some children may be able to place other features, such as cities and deserts, correctly.

◆ Laminate a copy of a world map and cut it up into jigsaw-size pieces, and ask the children to put it together. Some jigsaws can be cut into smaller pieces to increase the level of difficulty.

Further literacy ideas

◆ Revise the use of commas in lists and help the children to list the oceans, rivers and so on shown on the map.

◆ Investigate *ai* words, as in *plain*, and encourage the children to think of as many as they can, for example *train* and *rain*.

◆ Ask the children to write a story for which the setting includes one of the physical features on the map, for example a river or a mountain.

◆ Ask the children to write a description of a journey from one end of a continent to another. Advise them to detail the features they pass on their journey.

◆ Provide the children with comprehension questions about the map or get them to fill in a cloze passage. More able children could write their own questions about the map for a comprehension exercise.

◆ Help the children to use the contents and index pages of an atlas to find on smaller-scale maps some of the places you have looked at.

◆ Highlight some of the words on the map and ask the children to list them in alphabetical order.

◆ Use some of the longer and more unfamiliar words on the map to revise syllables, for example *Pa-ra-guay*.

◆ Use the map as a basis for the children to write facts in sentences, for example *The River Nile is in the continent of Africa.*

A house for sale

SmartMove
Property Services

New

Genre
information
with
persuasive
elements

End of terrace, Victorian 3-bed house. GCH.
Through lounge, dining room. Downstairs bathroom.
Ideal for first-time buyer.
Parking space.
Contact our office to view.

SmartMove
Property Services

Charming 4-bed s/d house.
Superb gardens. Garage.
Separate dining/sitting rooms.
Newly fitted kitchen.
A rare opportunity to buy in this area.
Close to local shops and railway station.
Viewing essential. Contact our office for appointment.

A house for sale

Geography learning objectives

◆ To express their views about places (1c).
◆ To use geographical vocabulary (2a).
◆ To make comparisons between features and places (3d).

Background notes

This text looks at house advertisements and the language used in advertisements, including some standard abbreviations. It also provides opportunities for looking at different types of house.

Vocabulary

Terrace, Victorian, lounge, bedroom, bathroom, buyer, parking, office, railway station, local shops.

Discussing the text

◆ Read through the text with the children and discuss any unfamiliar vocabulary, such as *terrace* and *ideal*. Look at the illustrations and go through some of the differences between the two houses. Can the children tell that the second one was built more recently than the first?

◆ Talk about abbreviations, for example *GCH*. Ask what these letters stand for and talk about why abbreviations are used (for example, to save space, to avoid repetition of commonly used terms). Can the children give other examples of abbreviations? Where have they seen them?

◆ Explain what the phrase *first-time buyer* means. Why do the children think that the first property might be ideal for this type of person?

◆ Discuss the language that is used to try to sell the properties – *ideal, charming, superb, newly fitted*. Can the children think of any other adjectives that could have been used in the advert? Brainstorm a list of words and phrases to describe each of the two houses, then see if there are any words that can be used to describe them both.

◆ *A rare opportunity*. Discuss this phrase and what it means. Do the children think that the estate agents are 'telling the truth'? What do we mean by 'telling the truth'? The estate agents cannot tell a 'lie', but that does not mean that they have to tell 'the whole truth', and they can choose their language carefully to embellish the truth, for example using phrases such as *ripe for modernisation* to describe a property that is probably in need of major updating.

Geography activities

◆ Ask the children to look carefully at the two houses and work out the differences between them. You will need to explain, possibly with the help of larger pictures, the various types of houses available, such as terraced, semi-detached, detached, flats, caravans. Which types of homes do these advertisements show? Ask the children to write a brief description of each house and list the similarities and differences.

◆ Why do people move house? See if anyone in the class has moved recently. Why was this? What happens to all the furniture? How does it all get transported? Ask the children to imagine that they could take only their two most precious possessions with them. What would they be and why?

◆ Look at pictures of houses for sale in your local area. (Estate agents will often give old photographs to schools.) Give each group of children a category of house, for example terraced or semi-detached, and ask them to collect examples of their type. Let the children choose one of the pictures of houses and write a short advertisement for it. What is it like and what would attract people to buy it?

◆ Look at the property pages in the local newspaper and ask the children to help you make a list of the good points made about the houses for sale. Why do people always put the best points about a house in an advertisement? Ask the children to draw their own home and make up an advertisement to sell it in the local paper. What are its best features? What would attract people to buy it?

◆ Discuss what makes a dream house. Do the children think they would like the same things as their parents? Ask them to draw their dream house, labelling the features they would like it to have.

◆ Use aerial photographs with the children to encourage them to look at buildings from a different perspective. What can they see from the air that they might not be able to see from the ground? Many postcards and pictures are oblique aerial photographs so children will already be used to seeing them. If there are any open spaces or fields on one of the pictures, can the children see evidence of any old buildings or pathways now covered over? Some television programmes have satellite images in their opening credits (for example, *EastEnders*). Look at these with the children to identify buildings and features such as rivers and open spaces.

◆ Using floor maps or large sheets of paper, ask the children to work in small groups to create a village or part of a town. Ask them to discuss what to put into the place and what sort of buildings go together. When the settlements are finished, ask each group to explain what they included and why.

Further literacy ideas

◆ Use the text to investigate compound words – for example *downstairs* and *bathroom*. Can the children list examples of other compound words that could be used to describe the inside or outside of a house, for example *fireplace*? This might be a piece of work that the children start at home.

◆ Use the text to revise syllables. Explain that the word *opportunity* has five syllables in it. Ask the children to clap the syllables as they say different words from the text aloud. Help the children to draw charts and record words from the text that have two, three and four syllables in them.

◆ Ask the children to write a story about moving house. Encourage them to write about how they feel about the move, what they are looking forward to and what they will miss.

◆ Write a list of comprehension/observation questions for the children to answer about the adverts, for example *How many windows can you see on the new house? Is this more or less than on the older house?* More able children could be asked to make their own list of questions.

◆ Ask the children to choose one of the houses to set a story in. Advise them to use some of the description from the adverts, for example it being Victorian, the local shops, the railway station.

◆ Ask the children to write labels and captions for one or both of the pictures.

◆ See if the children can change the text into more fluent, complete sentences, for example *There is an attractive four-bedroom house in the village with a lovely big garden.*

◆ Give the children a copy of the text with some of the words blanked out, for example *newly fitted* or *superb*, and ask the children to suggest suitable words for the spaces.

◆ In small groups, get the children to write a dictionary or glossary of 'house' words.

◆ Talk about the grammar and punctuation used in this type of text. How do they differ from those in fiction texts? (The shorthand style, incomplete sentences, no action, no narrator, present tense and so on.) Are there similarities? (For example, the prominence of adjectives.) Make sure the children understand the terms *fiction* and *non-fiction*.

◆ Use the word *room* to revise *oo* words like *foot, shook, good, moon* and so on.

Moving House

Genre
story in a familiar setting

The Sparks

This is the Spark family. Sam is seven and Sophie is five. They are moving into a new house soon.

The Old House

This is their old house. The Sparks sold it to Mr and Mrs Potts. The Potts have come to tea today.

At the New House

The next day, the Sparks go to see their new house. It needs painting before they can move in.

Two men from Cosy Carpets have arrived to put new carpets down in some of the rooms.

© Usborne Publishing Ltd

Moving House

Geography learning objectives

◆ To ask geographical questions (1a).

◆ To communicate in different ways (1d).

◆ To use geographical vocabulary (2a).

◆ To use secondary sources of information. (2d).

◆ To identify and describe what places are like (3a).

Background notes

Moving home is a traumatic experience for young children, as well as being very exciting. This extract is used as a starting point to look at why people live where they do and why people move.

Vocabulary

Move, furniture, house, terrace, detached, job, flat, bungalow, maisonette, buy, sell, services.

Discussing the extract

◆ Look at the headings only at first and see if the children can predict what the story is about.

◆ Discuss what is happening in the first two pictures. How many children in the class have moved house? Encourage them to talk about their experiences of moving house.

◆ How do the children think Sam and Sophie feel about moving house? What might make them happy or excited? What might they be sad about? Talk about things they might be worried about.

◆ On a board or flip chart, brainstorm all the people involved in the house move. What part would each person play?

◆ Discuss what the Sparks and the Potts might have talked about when the Potts came to tea.

◆ Cover the right-hand side of the final picture and text. Look at the rest and ask the children to imagine the conversations taking place at the new house. What is Mr Sparks talking about with the neighbour? What might Mrs Sparks be saying to the painter? What is Sam saying to Patch? Why?

◆ Talk about what might happen next. What will the rest of the picture show? What sort of thing do people have done straight away when they move in to a new house? Reveal the picture and see if anyone was right.

Geography activities

◆ Ask the children why people move house. (Changing jobs, nearer to family, need more room and so on.) Why do the children think the Sparks are moving house? What clues do the pictures give?

◆ What type of house are the Sparks moving from? What type are they moving to? What other words for houses do the children remember? Build up a list of words, then ask the children to label some pictures of houses with the correct types.

◆ What jobs are involved in moving house? (For example, buying and selling, arranging estate agents, solicitors, removal men, carpet fitters, painters and decorators.) Ask the children to list as many as they can.

◆ What information would be useful for someone moving to a new area? (The locations of shops, post office, playground, park, school, petrol station and so on.) Ask the children to imagine they are Mr and Mrs Spark writing a list of such information for the Potts.

◆ What would the Potts children like to know about the new place to which they are moving? Would they want to know the same things as Mr and Mrs Potts? Get the children to write a list by the Spark children for the Potts children.

◆ Talk about the various services provided to our houses. (Water, electricity, gas and so on.) Who would need to be told when people are moving? What happens to post sent to the old address? Ask the children to make a list of all the people who would need to know when people move house. As well as all the services, remind the children that friends and the rest of the family would need to know.

◆ When people sell their house, what information would potential buyers need to know? Ask the children to list the subjects in three categories: basic information about the house (number of rooms, their sizes and so on); more detailed description of the house (for example, the state of the garden); the local area (including amenities).

◆ Encourage the children to think of the different types of house in the local area. What services are provided to the area (including transport services)? Who pays for them? How are they paid for? (For example, by quarterly bills, council tax, bus pass.) Help the children to make a simple plan of one of the streets and join all the direct (fixed) services to each house. Ask them to make a list at the top of the street of all the other services, such as post delivery, buses, and waste collection, that do not have fixed connections.

◆ Explain to the children that houses may be owned or rented (or sometimes a combination of the two). What is the difference? Discuss the advantages and disadvantages of both. For example, when you buy a house you are paying for it as a way of 'saving' your money; on the other hand, if you rent a place then it is easier to move to another place if, for instance, a better job becomes available. Ask the children to work in pairs to make a list of the advantages and disadvantages of each after the discussion.

Further literacy ideas

◆ The children could give oral or written accounts of the move from the old house to the new.

◆ Let the children choose one or more of the people moving house and write a description of them. What do they look like? What sort of clothes are they wearing and so on?

◆ Ask the children to write about one of the animals that is moving house. Describe what it looks like, what sorts of things it does, what it likes to eat and how it should be looked after, and how it should be cared for particularly during and after the move – carried safely, settled into a new hutch or kennel and so on.

◆ Ask the children to make a list of nouns relating to the new house, for example *window* and *door*, using both the words and pictures from the text.

◆ Ask the children to write a couple of paragraphs for a compare-and-contrast passage highlighting the differences between the old house and the new one.

◆ The children could write a simple letter to a friend or relative telling them that they are moving. Remind them of letter-writing conventions and advise them to include details such as when the move will be taking place and the new address and phone number.

◆ Making a link to ICT and art and design, the children could design change of address cards.

◆ Use the text as a basis for exploring antonyms. Ask the children to make lists of opposites, for example *old – new; small – big.*

Finding your way around the park

Find your way round the park by following the directions below.
Draw your route as you go around.

- Start at the car park.
- Walk west to the south gate.
- Go north and then north-west to the wet weather shelter.
- Go north to the ice cream van.
- Go east to the duck pond. Sit down to enjoy your ice cream.
- Walk south-east to the litter bin to put the wrapper in.
- Go north-east to look at the flowers.
- Go south to the playground.
- Go east past the picnic tables and leave the park by the east gate.
- Go south to the car park.

How well did you do?

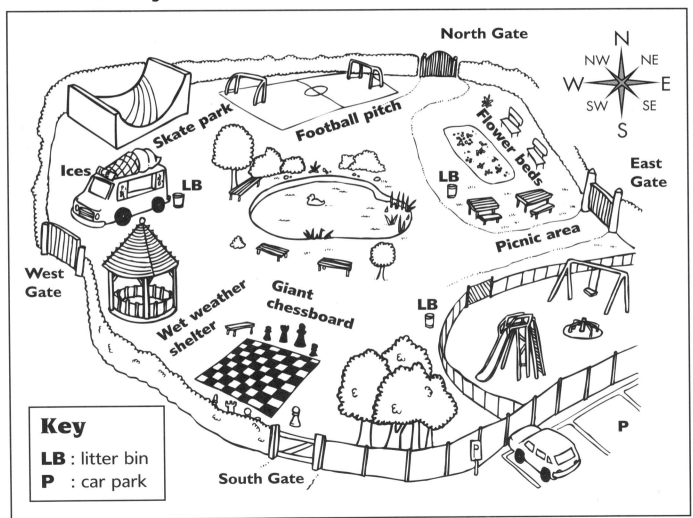

Key

LB : litter bin
P : car park

Finding your way around the park

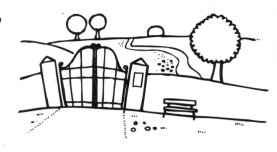

Geography learning objectives

◆ To recognise and use compass points correctly (1b, 2b, 2c).

◆ To give clear instructions and talk to adults about their work (1d).

◆ To carry out a geographical interview (1d, 2a, 2b).

◆ To identify where places are (3b).

Background notes

Following and giving directions are important skills for children to learn. This extract gives practice in both. It can be followed up with practical exercises around the school buildings and grounds, or on playmats or drawn maps.

Vocabulary

Benches, car park, shelter, picnic area, playground, pitch, swings, skate park, north, east, south, west, gate.

Discussing the text

◆ Show the text to the children and see if they recognise it as a set of instructions. Through shared reading, highlight the key words and phrases (for example *Start, car park, west, south gate*).

◆ Work through the instructions one by one and discuss whether or not they are 'accurate' (As in almost all cases when we use directions such as *north* or *south-west*, these are approximations.)

◆ What other lists of instructions have the children come across? Where were they? (For example, in recipes, how to play video games, what to do in a fire drill.)

◆ Discuss the text in terms of fiction and non-fiction. The park is an imaginary one and so is 'fictional', but can we categorise the instructions in the same way?

◆ Emphasise the order of the instructions. Does it matter in what order you read the directions? Is this the same with all instructions? Demonstrate why and how instructions must be in sequence and clear and unambiguous.

◆ Brainstorm directional vocabulary, including prepositions, for example *behind, in front, forwards*.

Geography activities

◆ Look at the layout of the park. What does it contain? How is it different from a garden? What are the various areas used for? Which of the park's facilities would the children like to use?

◆ Talk to the children about the points of a compass. It might be helpful to use a large class-sized compass to demonstrate the cardinal points. Why is it useful to be able to use compass directions? (It is clearer to say *north of the church* or *south of the river* rather than *behind the church* or *over the river* because the person receiving the instructions may be looking from a different direction than the person giving the guidance.) What other terms can we use when giving directions to people? (For example, *Turn <u>left</u> at…*)

◆ Ask the children to follow the directions around the park. Do the instructions work? How could they be improved? Working with partners, ask the children to work out a route of their own and then test it out on another pair.

◆ Get the children to assess the features and facilities in the park. What else could they add? (For example, toilets.) Why are there a fence and a hedge round the park? Do they think the park is always open? If not, when might it be closed? Who might use the park? Is there something for everyone? If the park was located in a large town, what might the children be able to hear and see from the park?

◆ Ask the children to practise writing directions for round the school building or the school grounds. Some children can use more basic instructions such as *left*, *right* and *straight on*, whilst others can use a simple compass to define the right direction. It might be helpful to give an example, such as *Leave the classroom, go north along the corridor, turn east at the junction and then west into the playground. What can you see when you look south?*

◆ Encourage some children to give more abstract instructions (from memory and knowledge, rather than following a map and without using the points of the compass) from school to a local feature nearby or to their home.

◆ Set the children the task of finding how well adults can explain a route. Ask the children in pairs to ask an adult to give directions from X-point to Y-point. This could be in the school grounds or further afield. (If working beyond the school grounds, this will best be done in groups with adult support.) Tape-record the answers and then play them back to see how clear the instructions are. Is giving instructions a difficult thing to do? Why? (We understand how to do something ourselves, but it is hard to break down the process to describe how to do it to someone else.) Ask the children to try explaining to their partners how to put their coats on or tie shoelaces. Make sure the person only follows the instructions and doesn't do the task instinctively.

◆ Suggest to the children that they design their ideal park layout. Brainstorm possible features they could and should include, then give out large paper to small groups and tell them they must discuss what they want to include before they go ahead and draw it in — it must be a corporate effort.

Further literacy ideas

◆ Ask the children to write a story set in the park. You could specify certain objects that have to feature in the story.

◆ Ask the children to describe a route through the garden noting what they pass on the way. Help them to put some of the instructions into a simple flow chart or diagram.

◆ The children could list directions for another route, for example from one end of the school to the other.

◆ Use the text as a starting point for investigating compound words for example *football, playground, chessboard*. Can the children see which smaller words are making them up?

◆ Help the children to turn some of the statements in the text into questions. Work through using *what*, *where* and *when*.

◆ Practise spelling words with the *ch* phoneme, such as *pitch* and *bench*.

◆ Ask the children to write a set of instructions for performing a simple task, for example making a sandwich or cleaning your teeth.

◆ Look at words that contain double consonants, such as *chess* and *football*. What others can the children think of? See if everyone can spell them and know their meanings.

◆ Cut out and mix up the individual instructions from the photocopiable sheet, and ask the children to reorder them in the correct sequence.

Genre
annotated
picture map
in the style of
an oblique
aerial
photograph

shop telephone

church

graveyard

Water tank

Shop

shop

Horta's house

un
ho

BUS

Living in Tocuaro

Most people in Tocuaro know each other. It is a very friendly place. The village has grown up on fairly flat land near a lake, although there are mountains not far away. Most farmers grow maize and beans. Some also grow lentils, wheat and alfalfa. Others own cattle which graze on the lush grass. Close to the lake the land can be very wet and muddy.

"Tocuaro is a very small place. Apart from the church and the school there are only a few shops."

BULL RING

Nursery

shop

"We like to play outside with our friends as it is pleasantly warm all year round. The roads are not very busy – so we can play safely in the street. There are lots of places to hide."

Tocuaro lies behind the road which circles Patzcuaro. Buses travel along this road linking together all the villages around the lake with the towns of Erongaricuaro and Patzcuaro. There are few cars in Tocuaro, but horses and donkeys carry firewood and maize between the houses.

"The nearest town to Tocuaro is Erongaricuaro which is six kilometres away. However most people travel to Patzcuaro (14 kms away) which is larger and has more shops and services."

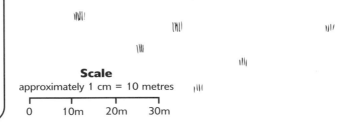

Scale
approximately 1 cm = 10 metres

0   10m   20m   30m

PHOTOCOPIABLE

Living in Tocuaro

Geography learning objectives

◆ To use maps and plans (2c).

◆ To identify and describe what Tocuaro is like (3a, 3b).

◆ To recognise how Tocuaro compares with where they live (3d).

◆ To learn about a locality outside the UK (6b).

Background notes

This text provides the children with an opportunity to learn about a locality outside the UK and can help to introduce a variety of places so that children's knowledge of the world is continually being extended.

The map is related to the QCA Scheme of Work at Key Stage 1 'A contrasting locality overseas – Tocuaro', but is based on the Key Stage 2 resources published by Worldaware. Tocuaro is a village in Mexico, about 400 kilometres west of Mexico City, with about 600 inhabitants.

Vocabulary

Village, lake, mountains, farmers, maize, beans, wheat, alfalfa, cattle, muddy, kilometres, firewood, donkeys.

Discussing the text

◆ Read the first section, under the heading, and check that the children understand all the vocabulary, including less familiar words like *lush* and *maize*. Demonstrate the pronunciation of the word *alfalfa* and use this as a starting point for a general discussion on pronouncing words from other languages.

◆ Ask the children to take it in turns to read the sections of text in inverted commas – spoken by children from Tocuaro.

◆ Point out the different styles of texts. Why do the children think there are different types of text? What is their impact? (It gives some variety to the text and also helps to indicate which items are more important than others. Can the children suggest other reasons?)

◆ Talk about the overall presentation of the text, the use of boxes. Do the children like this style of presentation? Have they seen similar presentation in any other texts? Talk about how non-fiction texts are more likely to be presented in this way than stories.

◆ Discuss what the children in the text say about living in this place. Would anyone in the class like to live here? Has anyone visited somewhere like this? Use the text to make a list of advantages and disadvantages of living in Tocuaro.

Geography activities

◆ Discuss the features of Tocuaro. Which would the children find in their locality and which are very different, such as the bullring? What is the landscape like? Is it a village or a town? What are the reasons for their decision?

◆ The children could investigate the daily weather in Tocuaro or Mexico City by using the BBC weather site: www.bbc.co.uk/weather/worldweather/index.shtml.

◆ Make a list of the physical and human features identified in both the picture and the text and, with the children's help, sort them into two lists on the board. For example, physical – hills, mountains, lake;

human – shop, village, house, fields. Ask the children to write an explanation of some of them or to compile a geographical dictionary, setting the words in alphabetical order.

◆ Ask the children to plan a route from one of the houses (for example Uncle's house) to another named place in or around the village. You may need to revise directions such as *right, left, round the corner, straight on, first*. The difficulty can be increased by asking the children to visit several places on one journey and plan a route that will not require them to retrace their steps.

◆ How do people travel in Tocuaro? There are several clues, both on the map and in the text. Are there many cars? Why not? How do the means of transport compare with those in the children's locality? Are there any that are similar? Give groups of children a Venn diagram on a large piece of paper. One set should be labelled *Transport in Tocuaro* and the other *Transport in our area*. Then ask the children to list all the forms of transport in the correct area of the Venn diagram.

◆ After the children have discussed the information, ask small groups to fill in a table to compare their area with that of Tocuaro. Use headings like *landscape, houses, transport, size, jobs people do*.

◆ Discuss this method of drawing a picture map. Does it give a good idea of what Tocuaro is like? Is it interesting and attractive? Ask them to draw a picture map of their own area to show the main physical features and buildings. If the children live in a large, built-up area they will need to discuss how far their map will cover. Are there any natural breaks or boundaries they can use?

◆ When they have talked about life in Tocuaro, ask the children to work out the questions they would most like to ask the people who live there. These can be written in the form of a letter to the Horta family who live in the centre of the village. Revise style points for setting out letters and give the children ideas on what else they should include – facts about themselves and information about where they live, for instance.

Further literacy ideas

◆ Use the words spoken by the children in the text to introduce or revise how speech marks are used when writing dialogue.

◆ Go through the text to complete a table with the column titles *What we already know* and *What we want to find out*. Follow this work by a shared or guided reading session to answer the questions.

◆ Demonstrate to the children in a shared or guided writing session how to make short notes from a text by selecting key words and writing the main words from a sentence or paragraph. Give the children a copy of the text and a highlighter pen and ask the children to make short notes. The children's findings could then be shared in a plenary session.

◆ On individual whiteboards, ask the children to experiment with different styles and sizes of font using ideas from the text. They could compare block capitals and ordinary lower-case writing with normal capitals where needed, as well as 'sloping' (italic) styles of both, and see which of them is easier to read, which looks most 'important' and so on. (In e-mails and Internet chat rooms, using block capitals is seen as 'shouting'. Can the children suggest why this is?)

◆ Ask the children to make a glossary to accompany the text that could be used by other readers. For example, they could find the meanings of and give definitions for words like *maize* and *kilometre*.

◆ Tell the children to imagine they are some of the children living in Tocuaro and to write a short account of what their life is like. Suggest that they think about anything they would like to change.

◆ Ask the children to write some descriptive statements based on the map and including directions. For example, *As you come away from the bullring, you will pass the nursery on your left-hand side*. Additionally, present the children with statements like this and ask them to turn them in to questions.

◆ Spend some time in shared or guided writing showing the children how the setting for a story can be built up from small details, and ask the children to write a short story set in Tocuaro.

The homecoming

From their viewpoint high above the town of Dolceacqua, Silvio and Carla had a bird's-eye view of the piazza lying below them. The river glinted in the hot sun. The cars in the street looked like toys as they moved along. Behind the children, the castle stood like a sentry guarding the hillside, casting its shadow on the town below.

"There it is," shouted Carla as the bus drove into the silent, sleepy square. "Come on Silvio!"

They scrambled down the rocks, past the castle gate, their feet clattering on the cobbled paths of the old town. The narrow streets, without any cars, made the sounds echo against the ancient walls. As they ran down, they disappeared into the cool, dark, shadowy streets, past shuttered houses and silent, watchful cats.

They burst into the hot sunlight of the piazza, where the stones were almost too hot to tread on. "Ciao Mama," they chorused to the figure standing in front of them. "Welcome home!"

Paula Richardson

The homecoming

Geography learning objectives

◆ To use geographical vocabulary (2a).

◆ To identify and describe where a place is and what it is like (3b, 6b).

◆ To understand how weather can have an impact on a place (3c, 4b).

Background notes

Dolceacqua is a small town on a bend in the River Nervia in the Italian province of Liguria, about six kilometres inland from the coastal town of Ventimiglia, very close to the border with France. It has a very old town centre of houses seemingly piled on top of one another and is dominated by its old castle. Newer buildings stretch a short distance up and down the valley from the old town.

Vocabulary

Viewpoint, piazza, sentry, shadow, square, cobbled paths, narrow, echo, shadowy, silent, ancient.

Discussing the text

◆ Show the children just the title of the story – 'The homecoming.' Can they predict what the story is going to be about? What or whom do they think is coming home?

◆ After shared reading of the text, ask the children where they think this story is set. Is it set in this country or abroad? What clues are there that the text might be set in another country? Do the children have any idea what country the story is set in?

◆ Point out the word *piazza*. What other word does it remind the children of? Is this a clue as to where the story is set? Do the children know of any other words that are commonly associated with other countries? (Other food examples might be *kebab, paella, smorgasbord*.)

◆ Go through the text looking for other words that tell about the setting for the story, for example *cobbled paths, shuttered houses*. Do any of these things tell us about how new or old this place is?

◆ Read through the story again and discuss with the children any time that they have been away from home and how they felt when they came back. On the other hand, have they ever been in the position of the children in the story and been waiting for someone to return home?

◆ Discuss the way the author describes the castle as standing *like a sentry guarding the hillside*. What effect does this have? Can the children think of a different way of describing the castle and the way it towers over the town?

◆ Talk about the punctuation used in the passage, in particular the speech marks and exclamation marks. Point out how speech marks are used when characters are talking. Role-play the passage with some of the children taking turns to play the parts of the children and their mother.

Geography activities

◆ Find clues together that tell us where the place is and what is it like to be there. Is it a flat place? What is the weather like? Ask the children to write a description beginning *Dolceacqua is…*

◆ Talk about the castle at the top of the town and the piazza by the river. Show some pictures of similar cobbled streets and narrow alleys if you can. Ask the children to draw the children's route down from the castle to the piazza, drawing in and labelling as many features as they can.

◆ Let the children use the Internet to discover what the weather is like today, and in other months, in this part of Italy. Compare it with home. Why do they think that a school like theirs in Italy is only held in the morning?

◆ Help the children to use an atlas to find where Dolceacqua is. Which country is it in and which other countries is it near? How could we get there from Britain? Which language will the people speak? Ask the children to look up Italy in a reference book and see what they can find out about it.

◆ What kind of Italian things do we have in this country? What about cooking? Talk about pizza and show the difference between this word and *piazza*, which means *square*. Ask the children if they have tasted pizza or other Italian dishes. Can anyone describe how pizzas are made? Ask a local restaurant for a menu and have a look at some of the types of Italian dishes they cook. Talk about the different types of filling and toppings for pizzas. You could help the children to make a pizza or to design one.

◆ Ask the children to imagine they are meeting someone in their town or village either at the train or bus station. They should write a description of what they saw on their way to the station. What did they pass and what was it like? They could set their story in a cold, wet, winter storm or a windy, autumn day. How did the weather affect the place and their journey?

Further literacy ideas

◆ Ask the children to imagine that they are the mother on the bus and tell them to write a few sentences about what she is thinking as her bus approaches the town.

◆ There are lots of excellent adjectives in the passage. Ask the children to mark some of these on a copy of the passage using a highlighter pen, for example *silent*, *sleepy*, *hot*, *cool* and *dark*. More able children could suggest alternative adjectives for some of the words, such as *quiet* and *burning*.

◆ Tell the children to imagine they are sitting on a hillside above the place where they live and to describe what they see below them. Are there roads? Is there a railway line or a river?

◆ Encourage the children to imagine they have been away from their friends or family for some time. Tell them to write a letter to a friend or family member, describing what they are looking forward to seeing and doing when they return.

◆ Use the comparison of the castle to a sentry on duty to introduce the children to simple similes. Can they find any others in the passage? (The cars like toys.)

◆ Help the children to highlight all the parts of the text that tell us something about the setting.

◆ Ask the children to continue the story. What do they think happened once Mama returned home? What did she and the children talk about? What did they do?

◆ Use a story planner to record the main parts of the story. Ask the children to use it to retell the story, either orally or in simple written sentences.

◆ Ask the children to create their own stories based on the text. Advise them that they should use the same setting and/or the same characters. Remind the children to plan their story with an interesting beginning, events in the middle and a satisfactory closure at the end.

◆ See if the children can write a short summary in the style of a book blurb to give people an idea of what the story is about.

◆ Ask the children to make a simple picture book for a younger child, retelling the story in pictures with simple statements.

Barnaby Bear in Brittany

Barnaby's Nan said they were going to a part of France called Brittany and would stay in the town of Roscoff. Grandpa got out a map and helped Barnaby to find these places.

Genre
information text and map using a fictional character

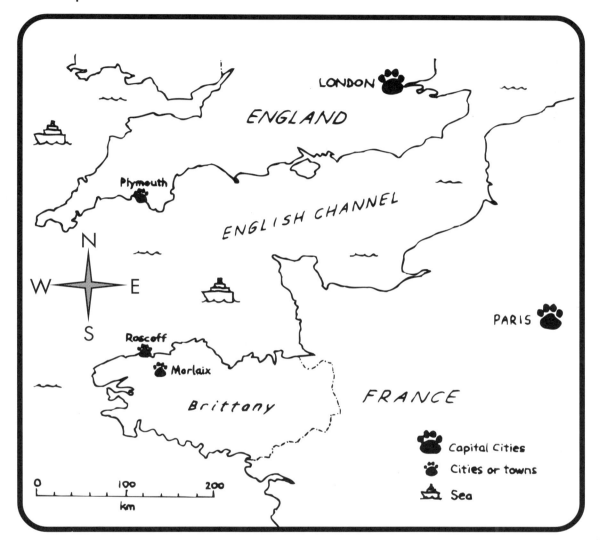

Barnaby noticed that there was a lot of water called the English Channel between France and England. He hoped he didn't have to swim across, as he had only just started swimming lessons!

Nan and Grandpa had decided not to take the car, so they would travel around Brittany by bus and train.

Elaine Jackson © The Geographical Association

Barnaby Bear in Brittany

Geography learning objectives

◆ To use geographical vocabulary (2a).
◆ To use maps and plans (2c).
◆ To use secondary sources to locate places (2d).
◆ To identify what a place is like (3a, 6b).

Background notes

This story of Barnaby Bear visiting France, introduces the concept of Europe to younger children and provides a basis for building a greater understanding of Europe in later years.

This text and the following two are based on the Barnaby Bear books and scheme of work.

Vocabulary

France, Brittany, Roscoff, English Channel, swimming, travel, train, capital city.

Discussing the text

◆ Read the beginning of the text through with the children and then talk to them about the map. Demonstrate to the children how to pronounce the names of the French towns – Roscoff and Morlaix.

◆ Talk about the text in terms of fiction and non-fiction. In this case, we have real places, but the story itself and its main character is fictional. Talk about the labels on the map. Why do the children think these are written in different fonts? Why are some words larger than others and why are some of them all in capital letters?

◆ Discuss the punctuation used in the text. Ask the children if they know what the punctuation mark in the first word is (the apostrophe) and why it has been used. Try reading the first two sentences with the children without putting in the full stop. How does this affect the reading of the passage? Talk about the exclamation mark and why it has been used in this text. Point out the comma in the last sentence on the page. What is the purpose of this? How does the sentence sound if you do not pause in the place where the comma is?

◆ Talk about the key on the map and ask the children why it has been used. How does a key work? Have the children seen a key before, where was this and what was the key representing?

◆ Talk about the compass on the map and revise the four main compass points. Draw attention to the scale bar at the bottom of the map and explain to the children how it is used to represent distances.

Geography activities

◆ Discuss with the class where Roscoff is in relation to Plymouth and to England in general. Look at a large map of Britain to allow children to work out where they live in relation to Roscoff and France. It will also be helpful to show where France is in relation to other European countries as well as the extent of the English Channel. Which are the nearest neighbours to both France and England? Can the children find places such as the Channel Islands and the Scilly Isles? Use the scale on the map to work out some approximate distances between places.

◆ Talk to the children a little bit about life in France. The people who live there speak French and drive on the other side of the road. France has a greater variety of weather than we do. Look at the map to think about why this is. (Partly because it is a much bigger country.) Buy some baguettes from the supermarket and try out French cheese or jams, all now easily obtainable from stores. Set up a role-play buying ingredients for breakfast and then preparing breakfast. (Many French children have brioche and hot chocolate for breakfast.) Or you could set up a café scenario and have the children role-play a number of different jobs – waiters, guests, barman, chef and so on. You might also talk about how more and more foods of 'foreign' origin are now appearing in our shops. Do the children think we might all be becoming more and more alike? (Because of common television programmes and multinational businesses that promote their images in countries all over the world.)

◆ Look at some French money and explain about a number of European countries all now using the same currency – the Euro. Why might this be easier in some ways? Why might the French people be sorry to see the French francs go?

◆ Introduce some simple words in French so that the children begin to understand that other countries use a different language to ours. Leaning a French song will be helpful as they can then perform this in assembly or to other classes.

◆ Ask the children to predict what Barnaby might see in Roscoff. Direct them to the clues in the text – it is on the coast, it is a town and they already know some of the French words he might use. What sort of weather will he have? Ask the children to search a weather website, such as www.bbc.co.uk/weather or www.metoffice.gov.uk. If they type in the school postcode they will also get weather for their area. They can compare the weather in both places for the same day. If a record is kept across several days, the children can look at similarities and differences between the two countries.

◆ Use the map to identify place locations by using the compass points, for example *Roscoff is ___ of Plymouth.* (South.) *The name of the capital city of France is ___ and it is ___ of Roscoff.* (Paris; East.) It would be helpful to support this exercise by revising the compass points on a classroom compass.

Further literacy ideas

◆ Go through the text to find the contraction *didn't* and make sure the children understand it is a shortened form of *did not*. Give the children a list of other simple contractions and ask the children to fill in a two-column chart, putting the full version of the word next to its contracted version.

◆ Ask the children to write a story about a journey that they have made with a close friend or member of their family. Ask: *Where did you go? How did you travel? What did you do when you got to the place?* Use a story planner and let them write the story over two or three days, making sure it has a good beginning–middle–end structure.

◆ Write down the names of ten places from a map of the local area. Ask the children to sort these names into alphabetical order.

◆ Dictate to the children a selection of words, including a number of proper nouns, and ask the children to write them out, putting in capital letters where they are needed.

◆ Ask the children to think of some questions for a friend about the text. For example, *What is the name of the strip of water between France and England?*

◆ Together, use non-fiction reference books to find out more about France. Ask the children to help you make a list of things we know already, things we want to find out, and then afterwards, a list of what we have found out.

Barnaby Bear to the rescue

Genre
advice in the
form of a story

Barnaby rushed back to his Dad. "Dad! Dad!" he shouted, "May I use your mobile phone? A little girl has fallen and hurt herself." Dad switched on the phone to check the signal was strong, and handed it to Barnaby.

Barnaby phoned the emergency services. The operator had a very pleasant voice.

What emergency service do you require?

The Mountain Rescue Team, please.

The operator put Barnaby through to a policeman, who took all the details for the rescue team.

Barnaby explained quickly and clearly what had happened. He gave very careful directions using his map and compass.

Elaine Jackson (text), Roland Piper (illustrations)
© The Geographical Association

TEACHERS' NOTES

Barnaby Bear to the rescue

What emergency service do you require?

Geography learning objectives

◆ To communicate in different ways (1d).
◆ To recognise how places are linked by common technology (3c).
◆ To make observations about where things are located (4a).

Background notes

This story is about Barnaby Bear who, when out on a walk with his dad, finds a small girl who has broken her ankle. He helps the rescue services to find and treat her. Aspects of PSHE and citizenship are included, such as taking and sharing responsibility, first aid and recognising when help is needed and being able to ask for it.

Vocabulary

Mobile phone, signal, emergency services, compass, directions, rucksack, rescue, mountain, operator.

Discussing the text

◆ Read the introductory paragraph and ask the children to work out what has happened in the story so far. Where do they think the story is taking place and how do they think that the little girl fell.
◆ Ask two children to play the roles of Barnaby and the operator. Read the first page of text through, with the two children reading the text in the speech bubbles. Discuss why there are speech bubbles around some of the words. (To show the words spoken by the different characters.) Talk about other examples where the children have seen speech bubbles, for example in comics.
◆ Ask another child to take the role of the policeman, and read the second part of the text through together. Try different children in the roles and re-read the whole text, modelling how the children can read the roles with appropriate expression. Talk about how the operator would keep very calm and speak slowly and how the person making the call might be anxious and a bit nervous.
◆ Why do the children think that the text says that the operator *had a very pleasant voice* and that Barnaby tried to explain what had happened *very quickly and clearly*. Talk about making emergency phone calls. Why is it important to speak clearly and try to keep calm?
◆ Point out Barnaby hanging his bag up for the emergency services to see. Why was this a good idea?

Geography activities

◆ Discuss with the children the type of environment Barnaby is in. What are the clues? (The clothes he wears, the call for mountain rescue services.) What is a mountain? What are the characteristics of this type of landscape? Show some picture of hills and mountains and make a list of the features on a flip chart. What kind of features would probably not be seen? (Many human features, such as housing, factories and roads, for example.) Develop the concept of remoteness and 'away from it all' – the aspects that attract people to go walking or climbing in such areas in the first place. What does this mean if someone has an accident? How might he or she be taken to safety?
◆ Look carefully at the clothes Barnaby is wearing. What sort of equipment would the children pack if they were going to walk in the mountains? They will need to think about the types of clothing, food, drinks as well as a first aid kit, map, whistle, mobile phone, and other suggestions.

◆ Do we dress in particular ways for different occasions? What influences our choice of clothes? Discuss with the class the appropriate clothes for a variety of venues, activities and weather, such as the beach, a town centre, walking to school on a rainy day, helping to clear out the garage or shed.

◆ The children could practise bandaging up an arm – it is not necessary to always use proper bandages, but act as if it were an emergency and use a tie or belt or turned-in coat or similar. Explain to the children that, if a casualty had to be left until help arrived, without moving him or her, it is important to keep the person warm. Ask the children how they might do this. If you have a sleeping bag or 'bivvy' bag (a kind of sealable, waterproof sack that can be bought from a camping shop), work out with the children the best ways to put a casualty in with minimum movement.

◆ Why is it important to carry a map and a compass? Remind the children what it might be like on the moors or mountain – lack of easily recognisable landmarks, poor weather conditions like mist or fog. Show the children a map of a place. (A scale of 1:50000 is a good one to use as it has lots of names and the maps tend to be in full colour.) Ask them to pick out places or features they can read. What do they think the blue and brown represents? If they can recognise blue for water, they can discuss how they might use this information when lost. How might it help them to know if they are going up- or downhill for example? Compare a map of a mountainous area with one showing lots of towns. What strikes the children as being the main differences?

◆ Show the children a compass. Why is it useful? What can it tell us? How do we normally find our way round a place? (Signs, personal knowledge of where to go, someone tells us or shows us the way or takes there.) Why would finding his way be more difficult for Barnaby on the mountainside? Ask the children to work out instructions for their partners to find a place in school. Ask the partners to test this out and see if they arrive at the correct place. This is a good opportunity to practise *right* and *left* as well as *behind, across, in front of, beyond, next to* and so on.

◆ Talk about the emergency services. What are they? (Fire, police, ambulance, coastguard, mountain rescue, cave rescue.) For each service, make a list of when the children think they would be used. How do we call up the emergency services? Why is it important only to call them when it is a real emergency? Why is it important not to rely on a mobile phone to make emergency calls? (A mobile phone can be very useful, but you cannot be sure that it will be able to get a signal in a remote area; also, you must make sure that the battery is fully charged. Of course, there are not usually public call boxes in remote areas, but the closest one will probably be shown on a map.)

Further literacy ideas

◆ Ask the children to write out the conversations between Barnaby and the operator and then the policeman, starting the words of each new speaker on a new line. In a guided writing session, more able children could be shown how to put speech marks around the words that are spoken.

◆ Ask the children to write a prequel to the story. What do they think has happened before this extract? Ask the children to describe the setting and the events leading up to the accident.

◆ Ask the children to write out a conversation that they might have if they had to phone and ask for the police following a burglary, or the fire service following the discovery of a fire.

◆ In small groups, ask the children to develop a role-play based on the text, taking the parts of Barnaby and the emergency service operators. They could try to set it in their own area and then go on to perform it to the rest of the class or even the school in assembly.

◆ Use non-fiction reference books to find out more about the emergency services. Give the children a writing frame in which to make their notes. Then ask them to write their notes up into full sentences. Some of the children could then read out their findings to the rest of the class and the different pieces of information could be collated together in a class book.

Genre
personal
documents

Barnaby Bear goes to Dublin

Boarding card

Seat No **22b**	Flight No **533**	Date **15 April**	
Destination **Dublin**	Flight time **11.30**	Boarding Gate	**24**

✈ *BEAR AIR*

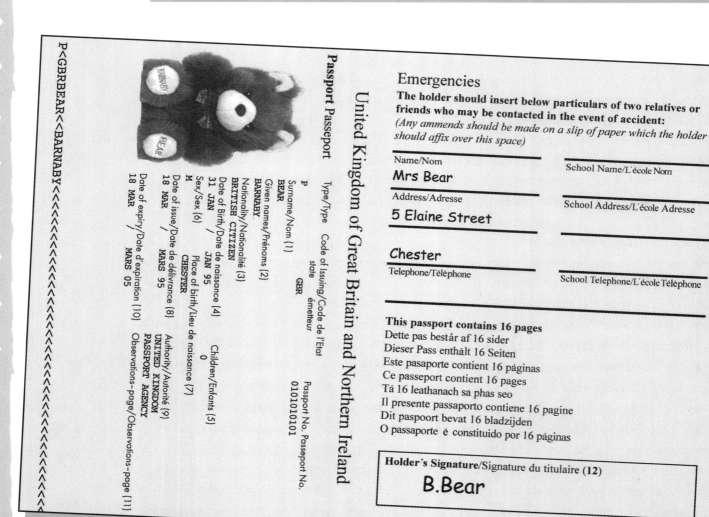

United Kingdom of Great Britain and Northern Ireland

Passport Passeport

Type/Type
P

Code of issuing/Code de l'Etat
state   émetteur
GBR

Surname/Nom (1)
BEAR

Given names/Prénoms (2)
BARNABY

Nationality/Nationalité (3)
BRITISH CITIZEN

Date of Birth/Date de naissance (4)
31 JAN / JAN 95

Sex/Sex (6)
M

Place of birth/Lieu de naissance (7)
CHESTER

Date of issue/Date de délivrance (8)
18 MAR / MARS 95

Authority/Autorité (9)
UNITED KINGDOM PASSPORT AGENCY

Date of expiry/Date d'expiration (10)
18 MAR / MARS 05

Children/Enfants (5)
0

Passport No. Passeport No.
010101010101

Observations-page/Observations-page (11)

P<GBRBEAR<<BARNABY<<<<<<<<<<<<<<<<<<<<<<<<<<<<<<<<<<

Emergencies

**The holder should insert below particulars of two relatives or
friends who may be contacted in the event of accident:**

*(Any ammends should be made on a slip of paper which the holder
should affix over this space)*

Name/Nom
Mrs Bear

Address/Adresse
5 Elaine Street

Chester

Telephone/Téléphone

School Name/L'école Nom

School Address/L'école Adresse

School Telephone/L'école Téléphone

This passport contains 16 pages
Dette pas består af 16 sider
Dieser Pass enthält 16 Seiten
Este pasaporte contient 16 páginas
Ce passeport contient 16 pages
Tá 16 leathanach sa phas seo
Il presente passaporto contiene 16 pagine
Dit paspoort bevat 16 bladzijden
O passaporte é constituido por 16 páginas

Holder's Signature/Signature du titulaire (12)
B.Bear

Barnaby Bear goes to Dublin

TEACHERS' NOTES

Geography learning objectives

◆ To use secondary sources of information (2d).

◆ To identify places and recognise jobs that people do (3a).

◆ To recognise how places are linked to other places in the world (3e).

◆ To know more about a distant place (6b).

Background notes

In this piece, Barnaby is going to visit the Republic of Ireland. We see his passport and boarding card for the flight. There is a link to PSHE and citizenship and the understanding of what it means to be a citizen of a country.

Vocabulary

Passport, citizen, agency, United Kingdom, emergency address, boarding card, gate, flight number, destination, Dublin.

Discussing the text

◆ Look at the two documents in terms of fiction and non-fiction. What sort of texts are they? What is a boarding card and when would you use one? Have any of the children ever seen or used a boarding card?

◆ Go through the different words and phrases on the boarding card. *Seat No* – what do the children think *No* stands for. Explain that it is an abbreviation for *number*. Discuss why abbreviations are used. Talk about *Destination* – what does it mean?

◆ Discuss why there are so many different bits of information on the boarding card. Cover up one piece of information, for example the flight time, and ask how this affects the boarding card overall. Are all the pieces of information necessary?

◆ Talk about the second document. Ask the children if they know what it is called. What is a passport? Do any of the children have their own passport? Talk about when a passport is used – not just for travelling, but also for identification. Go through the details that make a passport unique to just one person – the picture, the name and the number.

◆ Talk about some of the different languages used on the passport, for example *passeport* and the nine translations of *This passport contains*…. Can the children guess or work out any of the languages being used? Talk about why there are different languages on a passport. Give the children a few hints on this last point if they need them: *Why do we need a passport? Do we need one to travel in this country? Does everyone in the world speak English?*

Geography activities

◆ Discuss why Barnaby needs to use a passport. Where is he going? (Refer them to the boarding card if they have forgotten.) Where would we have to use one? Do we need one in this country? How can we prove who we are? Why might we need to do this? What sort of information does the passport tell us about Barnaby Bear? Would his photograph be the same for ever? Would ours be the same? Why might we have to use another photograph?

◆ Look at the boarding card. What is this for? Why must everyone have one before going onto the plane? Why is vital to know how many people are on the plane? What other documents do people have when going on holiday? Give the children a set of instructions, such as choosing a holiday, booking the ticket, going to the airport, checking in, going through passport control and boarding the plane. Muddle them up and ask the children to sort out the correct order in which they happen.

◆ Show a real passport to the children. What is the cover like? What does it say at the top? (European Community.) Explain Britain is part of a group of countries who link together for some activities such as buying and selling goods, sharing information, some legal procedures and working in some jobs. Some countries also share a common currency called the Euro, but in the UK we still have pounds sterling. However there are still some differences within the UK. For example, look at examples of £1 coins, which have different motifs, such as the leek for Wales and the thistle for Scotland. Some Scottish bank notes are different too.

◆ Use an atlas or large map to locate Dublin. Where is it? Is it inland or on the coast? What is the name of the river? (Liffey.) How would we get there? Which would be the quickest way for us to travel? Discuss the way the children could travel from school to Dublin. Look at the map together and ask the children to work out the best routes to take.

◆ Develop some role-play involving the use of passports and boarding cards. Set up a simple format with desks for check-in, places to queue, a passport check, boarding check in the departure lounge, and the aircraft seats arranged in twos and threes at one side of the classroom. Discuss what each person in a 'job' role will say. Appoint one person to give the 'welcome aboard' announcement.

Further literacy ideas

◆ Ask the children to make a passport for themselves or for a soft toy like Barnaby Bear. Give the children a template to fill in information like address, full name and date of birth. Revise the need for capital letters when writing names and places. Before starting this activity, the children could be given a copy of the text and could practise writing their address in the space next to Mrs Bear's.

◆ Point out the abbreviation of January on Barnaby's passport. Give the children a list of the months of the year and ask them to abbreviate them, for example March – Mar. The children could then arrange the months of the year in alphabetical order.

◆ Look at GBR under the country of issue and explain to the children that this is a commonly used abbreviation for Great Britain, although GB is also frequently used, especially in sporting contexts. Ask the children to find out and list what abbreviations are used for different countries for example NZ for New Zealand, NL for the Netherlands.

◆ Brainstorm a list of all the things you would need to do before going on a journey, for example packing a case, travelling to the airport or station, buying a ticket and so on, then ask the children to write a diary-style story about getting ready to go on a journey.

◆ Talk about initials, for example B. Bear in Barnaby's signature. What does the B stand for? Ask the children to write down all the first initials and surnames of the children in their group or class. They could then arrange them alphabetically – by first or last name.

◆ Use the passport as a starting point for teaching simple words in other languages. You could take a different language each day and ask the children to answer the register in that language.

◆ Give the children an enlarged copy of the sheet and ask them to list all the different words for passport, such as pasaporte, paspoort. They will probably enjoy trying to copy the Greek lettering. They could also compare how the word numbered is written in different languages.

◆ In a guided writing session, discuss what a signature is. The children could practise writing their signature on individual whiteboards.

Physical geography

CHAPTER
2

Physical geography deals with the land itself – the features that make up the landscape, the processes that formed it and the materials from which it is formed. It includes water processes and features as well as the weather and its processes and effects.

Children come to school with a lot of firsthand knowledge of the basic aspects of physical geography that are featured locally, although they will have a limited vocabulary to describe the features and little knowledge of how they came to be formed. In the same way, they will have a varied awareness of the weather.

The texts chosen for this chapter follow the themes of weather and water in various aspects and also look at some features of the landscape, both coastal and inland.

Work such as this should be supplemented by reinforcing the children's local knowledge by going out, looking at features and talking about what they see. The texts become more relevant when they are backed up by recent firsthand knowledge. Some of the texts also extend awareness by bringing in aspects of physical geography that will not be apparent in the local area and of which the children may have little or no experience, such as the Dales landscape in James Herriot's *Blossom Comes Home*.

Rain ➡ rivers and seas ➡ rain

Genre
information
diagram with
labels and
captions

Think about the water you use to bathe in and wash with.

It might have come from the Pacific Ocean or the River Nile.

It could have been used by trees and flowers to help them grow, and to raise crops like rice and wheat.

Water vapour forms clouds.

Rain

Sun's heat causes water to evaporate.

Rising water vapour

Rain ➡ rivers and seas ➡ rain

Geography learning objectives

◆ To use geographical vocabulary (2a).

◆ To identify and describe a process (3a).

◆ To recognise that places can change (4b, 5a).

◆ To recognise that places can be improved and maintained (5b).

Vocabulary

Rain, river, cycle, crops, water, precipitation, mist, snow, hail, sleet, drought, flood, lake, seaside, pollution.

Discussing the text

◆ Cover the words *Rain*, *Sun* and *Water* in the diagram before introducing it to the children and establishing that they have some idea of what it represents. Ask the children to suggest words that should go in the places you have covered. As the right words are suggested, ask the children which letters and sounds each word begins with and contains. Discuss the meanings of the words the children have provided and reinforce the spelling of each word to create a wordbank.

◆ Discuss the way the labels differ from 'ordinary' writing, for example they are brief and not always in complete sentences.

◆ Go through the diagram of the water cycle in more detail. How do we know where to start the sequence? What could we do to help the reader? (Perhaps number the labels or the arrows.) Is there a 'right' starting place? Emphasise that it is a *cycle*. Discuss how the pictures help the reader understand the labels and vice versa. Demonstrate other possible ways of labelling the diagram, perhaps including numbers and adding a key.

◆ Read the boxed text and find the River Nile and the Pacific Ocean on a map and/or globe. Talk about what continent the Nile is in. How might the water have got from there to our homes? (Think of the cycle: evaporation – wind blowing clouds – rain – river – reservoir – waterworks – taps.)

◆ Look carefully at the final sentence. The second part of the sentence is really covered by the first. Why is the part about rice and wheat included? What is the difference between the two uses? (The intention is to highlight 'natural' use of water, such as in the growth of 'wild' trees and flowers; and 'human' use of water – specific use for growing crops.)

Geography activities

◆ Discuss the way in which water is recycled around the environment. What would happen if some parts of the cycle slowed down or stopped, for example if no rain fell for a long time or fell continuously for days? Make class lists of the good and bad aspects of *no rain* and *lots of rain*.

◆ How does very wet, very cold or very hot weather affect us? How do we change our lives in relation to the weather? (Clothes, activities, bedtimes.) Ask the children to choose one of the situations and write a short story showing how we are affected.

◆ Suggest that there are different ways in which water (precipitation) can fall. How many can the children come up with? (Rain, hail, snow, mist, sleet.)

◆ Make a large copy of the diagram for display on the wall. Get the children to add information in the form of labels and captions, such as the different types of precipitation, water features (rivers, lakes, streams, the sea or ocean) and landscape features (hills, valleys, beach) to develop their vocabulary. These words can then be added to the wordbank.

◆ Use pictures of various water locations, such as lakes, rivers, seasides and discuss with the children how the places might be used for work, for example fishing, leisure activities, ferries, storage (reservoir). Then get the children to draw their own picture of a water location and identify the way in which the water area is used. Ask them to label and caption as many features as they can, using the vocabulary in the wordbank.

◆ Discuss how water can be polluted. How can we help to stop or reduce pollution occurring? (For example, making sure that we dispose of our rubbish in the right place, not tipping chemicals down the drain. Explain what we mean by 'chemicals' here. Bleach might be an example, but car oil could be another, less obvious one.) Is there a water feature near to the school? Is it tended? What state is it in?

◆ Use an atlas to look at some of the main water features of the world (seas, rivers and large lakes.) Do the children remember where the Nile is? Do they know any countries that grow rice or wheat? (Point out that some wheat comes from the Nile delta in Egypt.) Ask the children how water can 'move' round the world.

◆ Remind the children of the text, asking them to think about the water they use at home, and ask them to consider where it might have begun its journey. (It might have been a puddle you stepped in, or water in your fish tank.) Could the rain falling today have been rain falling 50 years ago? It is important to develop the children's understanding that all water, unless trapped, will sooner or later move around the water cycle.

Further literacy ideas

◆ Ask the children to write a sentence to go with each of the labels in the diagram, explaining what is happening at the different stages of the water cycle.

◆ Give the children copies of a picture of a house, garden or something similar and ask them to label the different parts. Tell them to include features such as a swimming pool or a play area that they would like to have. Share their labelled pictures with the class.

◆ Type out the different captions and labels from the diagram onto strips of paper and ask the children to sequence the sentences correctly.

◆ Ask the children to rewrite each of the following so it makes a proper sentence:

The falls rain.

Water rises vapours.

Evaporation heat causes.

◆ Ask the children to write down all the words from the wordbank (see Discussing the text) in alphabetical order.

◆ Let the children write a recount about an occasion when they went out when it was raining or were caught out in the rain, or when they got very hot.

◆ Ask the children which of the following words will take *-ing* and *-ed*: *rain, heat, rise, grow.* Can the children try this with some other common verbs that you give them?

◆ Using the diagram of the water cycle, encourage the children to write a story following a drop of water's journey from the Nile to their bath water.

What to do when it's sunny

Genre
advice/
instructions

It's very nice to see the sun and it means you can go out to play.
Sometimes in summer, the sun is very hot and too much of it can be bad for
you. The sun can burn your skin and make you feel very ill, so it's a good idea
to follow some simple rules to help you enjoy the sun.

Wear a hat and a top
when you are out playing.

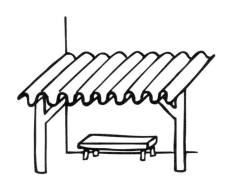

Use the shelter in the
playground at playtime.

Drink lots of water.

Don't stay out in the
hot sun too long – find
the shade.

Make sure you put on
some sun cream.

Don't run around and
get too hot in the sun.

Remember:
SLIP – SLOP – SLAP
Slip on a T-shirt – slop on the sun cream – slap on a hat!

SUN PROTECTION

Genre
fictional
information

Dr Xargle is an extraterrestrial who has written guides for other extraterrestrial visitors to Earth. Unfortunately, he often misunderstands what he sees...

Mad earthounds and earthlings go out in the mid-day sun. The earthlings strip to their underfrillies and rub each other with fat.

Then they lie on the floor in the shape of a star. When they go brown it means they are cooked.

Jeanne Willis (text) and Tony Ross (illustrations)

'What to do when it's sunny' and 'sun protection'

Geography learning objectives

◆ To identify and describe what places are like (3a).

◆ To understand how types of weather can affect what they do (3c, 4b).

◆ To recognise different types of weather (4a).

Background notes

People are far more aware nowadays of the dangers of too much exposure to the sun. These two texts look at this issue from serious and amusing standpoints. They use geographical material and also provide a useful link to work on PSHE where children are encouraged to understand the need to look after themselves when the weather is hot.

Vocabulary

Hot, cold, wet, rainy, sunny, sunburn, rule, forecast.

Discussing the text

◆ Go through the instructions in the sunny weather 'policy'. Why are we told to do these things? What happens if we don't drink lots of water or don't wear a hat?

◆ Introduce the term *rule*. Why do we have rules? What other rules do the children know about? (For example, the school rules, fire safety procedure.) Where are they found? How are they written, presented and displayed? Emphasise the need for clarity.

◆ Read through the Dr Xargle text and look carefully at the picture. Take the discussion on a more serious line and talk about the effect of heat on animals. What happens when someone needs to leave an animal in a car in hot weather? What should he or she do to ensure its safety?

◆ Through shared reading, highlight the key words or phrases in terms of weather and sun protection.

◆ Discuss which of the rules the children think is most important. Is it possible to put them in an order, or are they all as important as each other?

◆ Ask for suggestions as to how the negative sentences can be changed into positive ones, for example *Make sure you stay in the shade when it is very hot*.

Geography activities

◆ Talk with the children about the different types of weather and how these affect what everyone can do. Why does rain make life more difficult for us? Why is everyone in this country usually pleased when the sun shines? How do we feel in different types of weather?

◆ What are the good and bad things to do with sunny weather? Why is too much sun sometimes a problem for us? Talk about balance and explain the need to have rain and sun for plants to grow, while too much will cause floods or burning up of the plants.

◆ Discuss how too much hot weather can be dangerous for everyone. Ask the children to list ways in which they can still enjoy the sun, but keep themselves safe and cool. (For example using beach or garden umbrellas or the shade of trees, drinking water.) They can think about how this would apply at the seaside, for example, where they are more likely to be without T-shirts on the beach. Why are sunglasses a good idea? What about people who already wear glasses?

◆ The 'Sun protection' illustration shows people sunbathing. Can we only get sunburn when we sunbathe or can it happen at other times? Encourage the children to think about playing on the beach or in the paddling pool. What about other times at school, such as sports day? If the sun is hot, how does this affect everyone? Consider the spectators as well as the participants. In groups, get the children to discuss and note down as many occasions as they can think of in which there is danger from the sun and, in each case, how harm can be prevented.

◆ In which months can we expect hot weather like this in this country? What might we expect in the rest of the year? How can we find out what the weather is going to be like? Organise the children into groups and, for a week, they could: make a collection of various ways of showing the weather for the same week; record the weather at school; collect the newspaper records; watch television weather forecasts; use the Internet to look up information on a site such as Metlink (http://atschool.eduweb.co.uk/radgeog/MetNetEur/MetNetEur.html). At the end of the week, compare all the different evidence collected. Which forecast was the most accurate? Did the results represent the weather for all the day or just part of it? Should we trust the forecasts?

Further literacy ideas

◆ Look at *SLIP – SLOP – SLAP*. Use this phrase to introduce the concept of alliteration. Ask the children if they can think of any other phrases that alliterate like this.

◆ Ask the children to write a simple first-person story entitled *Out in the sun*. Encourage the children to write about things they have done or could do and to try to include some of the rules discussed. For example, *Before I went outside I made sure I put on my hat.*

◆ Look at *star* and revise *ar* words, such as *car, far* and *are*.

◆ Remind the children of the words we use for questions. (*How, why, what, when, where, who.*) Practise turning statements into questions and ask the children to write questions from 'What to do when it's sunny'. For example, *Why should you drink lots of water?*

◆ Investigate synonyms and words or phrases that express similar meanings. Give the children a number of words from the texts and ask them to write down synonyms on their whiteboards, for example *earthound – dog.*

◆ Let the children write a short story about the character who is sunbathing in the story. Advise them to choose whether she does or does not obey the sun-care rules.

◆ The children could write a story using the setting in the picture. Encourage them to include quite a detailed description of it at the beginning.

◆ Ask the children to use ICT packages to create a poster of the sunny weather advice, to be displayed in the school.

◆ Through shared writing, write a letter to parents or other children in the school, telling them what to do to keep safe when it is sunny.

◆ If you have them, read this and other Dr Xargle books (Red Fox), and discuss the humour. What makes them funny? (The different perspective and misunderstandings, as well as the funny, 'made-up' vocabulary used.)

Genre
*story in a
familiar
setting*

The wind blew

The wind blew.
It took the umbrella from Mr White and quickly turned it inside out.
It snatched the balloon from little Priscilla and swept it up to join the umbrella.

Pat Hutchins

The wind blew

Geography learning objectives

◆ To use geographical vocabulary (1a).
◆ To understand that there are different types of weather (4a).
◆ To recognise some of the effects that weather can have (4b).
◆ To recognise that we need different clothes for different weather (4b).

Background notes

Children get very excited by the wind. This text looks at the wind's effect on people and looks at another aspect of the weather. Work on the wind also has links to other curriculum areas including science and PSHE (such as recognising the need for different clothes for different weather).

Vocabulary

Wind, gale, storm, weather, blow, howl, whistle, gust, breeze, seasons.

Discussing the text

◆ Cover up the text and look at the picture with the children. Draw their attention to the effect the wind is having on the trees and the grass.
◆ Examine the picture in more detail and see if the children can identify other weather features. For example, Mr White is carrying an umbrella, so it is probably raining.
◆ Ask the children to suggest suitable text for the picture.
◆ Show the children the first line of text, *The wind blew*, and encourage them to predict the next lines. What might the wind do? Then uncover the rest of the text and compare it with the children's suggestions.
◆ Discuss the children's own experiences of occasions when the wind has blown quite strongly. Where were they and what happened? What other weather conditions did they notice?
◆ What do the children think the characters might be saying? Re-cover the text and ask the children to suggest text for speech bubbles to put on the picture.
◆ Use the text to practise reading with appreciation of punctuation. Demonstrate pausing where sentences end at the full stops. Show the children how this is important in making sure they understand what they are reading.

Geography activities

◆ Discuss with the children what *the wind* means to them. What words do they know for the wind? (For example, *breeze* and *gale*.) Make a list on the board or flip chart. Talk about 'moving air' and get them to link this concept with the wind.
◆ How do we feel when it is very windy? Get the children to describe what it feels like to be out in the wind. Is it easy to walk against a strong wind? Can you stand still easily in a gusty wind? What is a *gust*? (When we speak of a gust we usually mean a sudden, but short-lived, stronger wind – gusty conditions suggest that the wind strength is changing frequently.)
◆ Talk about the picture. What is happening to the people and what they are carrying, and to the trees? If the wind continues to blow very strongly, what might happen to the trees? Discuss the kind

of damage strong winds can do to the natural environment and also to buildings and high-sided vehicles or caravans.

◆ What time of the year might it be? It is not winter, because the trees have all their leaves. The man looks too warmly dressed for summer. If it were late autumn then the wind would blow leaves from the trees. In early spring the trees would be in bud. Perhaps it is late spring or early autumn.

◆ How do we dress on a windy day? Is it always cold when it is windy? (No, but the temperature usually feels lower in a wind than in still air.) Develop the discussion to include other types of weather and try to get the children to identify 'good' and 'bad' things about each. For example, *sun* – warm, pleasant to be outside, helps plants to grow… but danger of sunburn, drought kills plants, danger of forest fires; *rain* – need water for plants to grow, for our own use… but floods wash soil away, destroy houses and trees.

◆ Talk about the sorts of weather we expect at different times of the year (seasonal weather), for example snow. Does it *only* occur in winter? Do we *always* get such weather then?

Further literacy ideas

◆ Ask the children to suggest further words that rhyme with the words in the poem, for example *blew – flew, swept – kept,* and then get them to try to write a short poem using some of their suggested new words. The new poem would have the same rhyming pattern as the original, but the rhythm and meaning would probably be quite different.

◆ Use *The wind blew* as a story starter and ask the children to write a new story based on the Pat Hutchins model. Or the children could write similar stories with slightly altered story starters, such as *The snow fell* or *The sun came out.*

◆ Find the consonant clusters in the text – *bl, br, sn, sw* and practise reading, saying and spelling them. You could also look at the double letters in *umbrella, balloon, little* and *Priscilla.*

◆ Point out the long *oo* sound in *balloon.* Practise saying this and encourage the children to think of other words with this or a similar sound, for example *spoon, room* and *look.*

◆ Discuss letter patterns and sounds, such as *Priscilla* and *umbrella.*

◆ Ask the children to produce labels or captions for the picture, briefly describing the action and the changes that the weather is causing.

◆ Brainstorm adjectives that can be used in describing the setting for the story.

◆ Over three days, help the children to write a simple story set in this place, making sure they have a clear beginning, middle and end.

◆ Ask the children to create some more characters and objects to go with the pictures. Describe the characters and how the wind affects them.

◆ Compose a simple cloze procedure about the text, by omitting key words that the children have to supply, for instance, the name of the person who lost their umbrella, or the name of the object that was lost.

◆ Discuss words and phrases that could link these sentences, such as *First* and *then.*

FOUR SORTS OF EARTH WEATHER

Genre
fictional
information

Dr Xargle is an extraterrestrial who has written guides for other extraterrestrial visitors to Earth. Unfortunately, he often misunderstands what he sees...

There are four sorts. Too hot. Too cold. Too wet and too windy.

Unlike us, earthlets are not waterproof. They go soggy in the rainblob. They must put on a loose plastic skin.

Jeanne Willis (text) and Tony Ross (illustrations)

Four sorts of Earth weather

Geography learning objectives
◆ To recognise different aspects of our weather (4a, 4b).
◆ To recognise how weather can affect our lives (4b).
◆ To consider the effects of extreme weather (4b, 5a).

Background notes
This extract is taken from *Dr Xargle's Book of Earth Weather*. He has obviously listened to people (perhaps typical British people!) discussing the weather! This text brings together many of the weather and seasonal themes discussed in previous texts.

Vocabulary
Extreme, hot, cold, wet, windy, storm, hurricane, gale, downpour, heatwave, freeze, waterproof.

Discussing the text
◆ Go through the text and pictures with the children. Discuss who Dr Xargle is and who he has written his books for. Who are *earthlets*? Look at the other strange vocabulary – *rainblobs* and ask the children if they can think of alternative words.
◆ Look at the first picture and text again. Can the children tell you which description goes with which picture, for example *too windy*?
◆ Look at the second picture and re-read the text. What do we understand by what Dr Xargle refers to as *a loose plastic skin*? If necessary, direct the children to the raincoat in the picture.
◆ Carefully read the word *waterproof* together. What does it mean? Can the children find something or someone that is waterproof in the picture? Ask them to suggest other things that are waterproof.
◆ Look at the expression on the girl's face in each of the four parts of the first picture. How might she be feeling each time? Why?

Geography activities
◆ Discuss what the extract is about (it is only mentioned in the title). Talk about each of the mini-pictures in turn. Ask: *What does the picture show? Do you like this kind of weather? Why? Why not? Do you think other people like this kind of weather? Who might like it? Who might not like it?*
◆ Look at the second picture. What sort of protection do we need in the rain? What about the characters in the picture? This includes the dog with its soggy fur and the duck – designed for water, with naturally oiled feathers. How effective is each type of protection and in what circumstances would you use it (for example, 'emergency' protection from the newspaper)?
◆ Using the top two mini-pictures and the second picture, discuss how we dress for different kinds of weather and why. (For protection, warmth, to keep cool, to be comfortable.) Then give groups of children a weather type and ask them to draw themselves suitably dressed for it.
◆ Which are the children's favourite types of weather? Ask them to write some notes on why they like this weather, what they do during it and how they dress for it.
◆ Point out the repetition in the extract of *too*. Is this really true? Is the weather always too much one way or another? Talk about perceptions and that for people who are never happy with the

weather it *is* always *too…* Get the children to think about the effects of extremes of weather, such as drought, being 'snowed in', closure of roads, icy conditions, floods, trees blown down, buildings damaged and so on.

◆ Do we have any of the 'extreme' weather conditions discussed above? Are the occurrences frequent? Which ones occur most often? Is this the same for other countries? What might be the most extreme effects in other places, such as very hot or cold climates like tropical parts of Africa and Asia, or Siberia? Help the children to compare our heavy rains and strong winds with the tropical cyclones and hurricanes of the Caribbean and parts of the Pacific, and monsoon countries like India. Then make a chart with two columns – *Here* and *Another country*, and for each extreme, get the children to suggest the effects in this country and then in another country (naming the specific country or area in each case).

◆ How do people cope with extreme weather in other places? Explain that heavy snow occurs every year in certain places; in others, there is a very hot, dry season every year. In these cases, people adapt their way of life to conditions as they become 'normal'. What we consider extreme is not necessarily so for them. For instance, countries that have heavy snow each winter have equipment to clear roads and runways, special winter tyres for cars and so on – even understreet heating in cities to help keep the roads clear. Such investment would clearly not be affordable in most of the UK; nor, unlike parts of the USA, do we need to bother with tornado shelters. Stress, however, that extremes or rare weather events can disrupt daily life anywhere. In pairs, get the children to write a short piece starting *If we had cold snowy winters…* and then describe what preparations they would make for coping with the winter.

Further literacy ideas

◆ Using the four pictures of the weather, get the children to write one or more descriptive sentences to accompany each picture.

◆ Remind the children of the text's use of *too.* Can they see another *oo* word in the text? (*Loose.*) Ask them to list other words that contain *oo*.

◆ Give each child one or more of the pictures and ask them to write labels for it, describing the type of weather and what the people are doing and wearing.

◆ Re-read *Too hot. Too cold. Too wet and too windy* and ask the children to write full sentences containing each of these descriptions.

◆ Remind the children of the discussion on what the little girl might be thinking each time in the first picture. What might she say? Ask the children to write a speech bubble for each situation.

◆ Ask the children to choose one of the words in the text and find other words that rhyme with it, for example *wet – vet, pet, met*.

◆ Show the children that *four* contains the smaller word *our*. Can they find in the text any other small words inside larger ones?

◆ Ask the children what colour the raincoat might be. Then ask them to write for a friend some more comprehension questions about the pictures.

The volcano

Silvio and Carla were staying in Sicily with their grandmother for the summer holiday.

One morning, just as they were getting ready to go to the beach for the day, they were startled by the noise of a very big explosion. Rushing outside and staring upwards, they saw a black plume of smoke rising into the sky from the mountain top. As they watched, a red river of lava raced down the mountainside, flowing over rocks and snapping off any trees in its path.

Suddenly the air was filled with swirling pieces of ash and fragments of hot rock that landed everywhere. "Ouch!" said Silvio as a piece of ash landed on his arm. The air became dark and the birds fell silent. All that could be heard was the distant roar of the river of lava as it poured down the mountainside.

"Silvio, Carla, come inside!" cried their anxious grandmother. "Well, we certainly can't go to the beach today! We'll have to pack some things quickly and move out to somewhere safe!"

Paula Richardson

Genre
short story

The volcano

Geography learning objectives

◆ To recognise the extreme forces produced in a volcanic eruption (4a, 5a).

◆ To recognise that an eruption has a severe effect on people living nearby (5a).

Background notes

Volcanoes are awesome occurrences and children are fascinated by them. This short story brings out some of the thrill of firsthand experience. It introduces the children to an aspect of physical geography found in other countries and relates it to the lives of people living there.

Vocabulary

Volcano, erupt, lava, fragments, plume, smoke, ash, crater, mountain, gases, molten, active, dormant, Sicily.

Discussing the text

◆ Read the text through with the children, making sure that they understand all the vocabulary.

◆ Talk about the setting for the story. Make a note of all the words in the text that tell us something about the setting. In addition to the mention of Sicily, are there other clues that this story is not set in this country? (The volcano.)

◆ Point out the speech marks and read the text through, with two children taking the roles of Silvio and his grandmother. Discuss the appropriate expression for reading these words. Experiment with reading the story with different intonations. Demonstrate how the way you read the story affects the impact it has or how it is understood.

◆ Ask the children to imagine what might happen to the story if the setting were changed. Can they suggest settings for a similar story, for example near a river that bursts its banks?

◆ Re-read the text and identify the main events and the order and times at which they happen.

◆ Talk about how the writer uses descriptive vocabulary to help the reader build up a picture in their mind, for example *swirling pieces of ash and fragments of hot rock*. Encourage the children to suggest alternative and effective descriptive vocabulary that could have been used.

Geography activities

◆ Show the children pictures of volcanoes – both active and dormant, if possible. Ask them to describe how each one is different. What happens when a volcano erupts? What effects does it have on a place? What sort of noises would be heard?

◆ How would the eruption affect the area? (Darken the sky, cover everything in ash, send fragments flying, burn things.) What would the lava do to plants, trees and even houses in its path?

◆ Show the children some samples of volcanic rocks and lava. Ask them to feel them and weigh them. Rocks from an igneous base include basalt (hard), obsidian (shiny), granite (flecked pink), pumice (grey and light) and lava itself (with holes in it). How do they differ from each other? Let the children use samples, or refer to reference books, to find out more about each type. Make a chart to compare the rock types or ask the children to make a list of the attributes of each type.

◆ You could take the children for a walk round the school or the local area and ask them to list the types of rock they see and the ways they are used. (For example, granite – a building stone, slate – on pathways and roofs, limestone – in cement – sandstone – for building, cement blocks – from limestone and shale.) As with any fieldwork, you will need to prepare the route and identify the materials beforehand. Extend this by marking on a plan of the school or the local streets the places where rocks or stones are used in the environment.

◆ The children could list all the building materials used in the school and its grounds. Then ask them to work out which material is the most frequently used. What other materials are used in their area? Are there any modern developments to consider? Would their lists of building materials be different if they lived in another part of the country? Link to the text by asking, for example, if we find volcanic stone in this country.

◆ For some children, it will be appropriate to introduce them to the idea of the three rock types: igneous – formed through fire or heat; sedimentary – formed by deposits, usually in water; and metamorphic – rocks that have been changed. Ask them which type is most likely to be formed from a volcanic eruption, or in a river.

◆ Look at a world map showing physical features and ask the children to identify some famous volcanoes. Mount Etna is the one on Sicily, which erupted in July 2001. Another famous one is Vesuvius, across the Bay of Naples (for which excellent satellite images are available from, for instance, MJP – you will probably have a catalogue in school).

◆ Tell the children the story of Pompeii and Herculaneum and how the volcanic ash and lava from Vesuvius destroyed the towns in AD79. Ask them to find pictures and information about volcanoes and Pompeii from suitable books in the school library.

Further literacy ideas

◆ Brainstorm lists of words that might be used to describe volcanoes. Then use these with the story as a starting point for a shape poem entitled *The Volcano*. It might be helpful to show the children some pictures of volcanoes erupting to help them visualise such an event in their minds.

◆ Remind the children that Silvio and Carla were on holiday. Ask the children to write a story about an adventure they had when staying with a friend or relative during the school holidays, or to invent one if they don't remember or didn't experience any adventures.

◆ Use the phrase *startled by the noise* to encourage the children to use interesting vocabulary in their writing. Go on to find alternative words for *startled*, for example *shocked, surprised*. Write up these suggestions, then brainstorm words that describe things that might startle us, for example a noise: *bang, boom, roar, flash, crash* and so on). Display these lists on the wall for future reference.

◆ Encourage the children to use the Sicily setting to write another story.

◆ Ask the children to role-play the story in groups and perform it to the class. Tell them to think about what happens next in the story. More able children may be able to write a simple playscript for the story and its sequel.

◆ Ask the children to continue the story in prose. Provide them with a story planner so that they can be clear what is going to happen and in what order before they start writing.

◆ Help the children to write a few sentences that summarise what the story is about, in the style of a book blurb.

◆ Take the opening sentence of the second paragraph from the text and use it as a story starter, with different characters and a different setting.

◆ Look for all the verbs in the text, for example *getting, rushing, staring, watched*. Ask the children to work out what the root to the word is each time, for example *getting – get*.

◆ Use words from the text to investigate *oar* and *our* sounds (from *roar* and *poured*). Can the children think of any other words that contain these letter patterns and have similar sounds?

Genre
story in a familiar setting

Blossom Comes Home

I arrived at Mr Dakin's farm just outside Darrowby on a warm April morning. The green hillside ran down to the river, and the spring sunshine danced on the water. The birds were singing and the lambs played on the flower-strewn pastures.

Blossom Comes Home

Geography learning objectives
◆ To recognise the features of a UK farming environment (3a).
◆ To understand that people contribute to the character of the landscape (3c, 5a, 5b).
◆ To understand that there are different types of farm (3d).

Background notes
This text looks at a pastoral scene in the Dales. Blossom is one of the farm animals that has been with the vet and is now being brought back to the farm.

Vocabulary
Hill, farm, farmhouse, animals, crops, grass, pasture, meadow, field, sheep, cow, pig, moorland, valley.

Discussing the text
◆ Read through the text together and ensure the children are making the connections between the illustration and the descriptions of the setting. Go through any difficult vocabulary.
◆ Focus on the image of sunshine dancing on the water. Discuss why the author describes the sunshine this way. What other words might be used to describe the sunshine on the water? This could be extended to talking about words we could use to describe, for instance, flowers or trees in a breeze or a gale.
◆ Discuss why the narrator might be visiting the farm. What sort of people would visit a farm, and why? Direct the children's attention to the car as a clue. Then give the children the background to the story, explaining the *Blossom* in the title.
◆ Talk about the sounds you might hear if you were in this place and link this to work on the senses. Sounds might include the wind, work on the farm, farm animals and also wild animals, such as birds. Ask: *Do you think you might be able to hear aircraft? What smells might there be?*
◆ Discuss where the story is set. Is it in this country? Show the children the Dales area on a map. Have any of the children been to somewhere like this? What was it like?
◆ Draw attention to the narrative voice, the author's use of the first person.

Geography activities
◆ Ask the children to describe the landscape in the picture. Is it hilly or flat? What natural features can be seen? (Hills, a valley, river, moorland.) What features have been made by 'man'? (House and farm buildings are obvious, but it may not immediately occur to the children to classify fields as 'constructed' by people.)
◆ The farm in the picture has a lot of grass – pasture and meadow for the animals. Make a link to the children's learning on weather and explain that the sheep go up on the moorland in summer and are brought down for the winter season. Why do the children think this is?
◆ Ask the children to think of words other than *warm* which could be used to describe the weather in the picture.
◆ Ask the children if they have ever visited a farm. What sort of farm was it? Did it have animals? Were there different types of animal or only one? What is produced on farms? (For example, cereal

farming.) Do all farms grow crops? What do farms have animals for? (To produce meat, or milk or wool as well as some meat.) Ask the children to list all the animals that we might find on farms in this country and the products we get from them. (The main animals are cows, sheep and pigs, but deer, chickens and others are sometimes found.)

◆ The picture shows a farm in hilly countryside. Are all farms in hill country? Ask the children to think what the differences may be between farms in hilly country and lowland farms. (Lowland farms, with flatter countryside, tend to have better soils and can be ploughed, so various crops can be grown as well as animal husbandry being carried out. In hilly country, on the other hand, soil tends to be poorer and rather thin and stony. Ploughing is impossible on steep slopes. These conditions lead to hill and upland farms specialising in animal husbandry.)

◆ Ask the children to make a list of crops that are grown on farms in this country. This discussion can extend beyond the 'obvious' cereal or grain crops. Advise them to consider where carrots, potatoes and so on come from and include crops such as sugar beet.

◆ Talk about what animals eat. Is grass a crop? Explain that animals eat grass in the fields as part of pasture. The farmer also grows grass in meadows for hay or silage for winter feed, so it *is* a crop in the same way as the others.

◆ How many of the children have been for a walk in the countryside? Did they see any farms? Why do they think farmers ask walkers to keep to the paths? Refer to the discussions on crops. Would farmers like their crops trampled? If the children live in the countryside, get them to discuss the sort of advice that people from towns would need about the countryside and write their own Country Code for visitors.

Further literacy ideas

◆ Re-read *The green hillside ran down to the river*. Ask the children to look at the picture and make a list of the colours that could be used in the illustration.

◆ Ask the children to list all the months of the year and then to sort them into alphabetical order. Get them to use the Look–Say–Cover–Write–Check method to try to spell some of them. See if the children notice any similar letter patterns in them, for example Octo*ber*, Septem*ber*.

◆ Use the words *Dakin*, *Darrowby* and *April* to revise the use of capital letters for proper nouns.

◆ Ask the children to list the adjectives used in the text and to try to think of some more that would fit the picture.

◆ Use the text as a story starter. Ask the children to think about what might have happened when the car arrived at the farm. How was Blossom welcomed? How did she behave?

◆ *The birds were singing*. Get the children to list the sounds that other animals make and suggest other descriptive words for describing them.

◆ Mix up the three sentences and ask the children to sequence them correctly.

◆ *Hillside* is a compound word. Discuss what these are and ask the children for other examples. If they have recently read it, remind them of *waterproof* and *rainblob* in 'Four sorts of Earth weather' (see page 50).

◆ Use role-play to act out in small groups the narrator's arrival at the farm. What do the children think is said?

◆ Investigate simple and more unusual plurals, for example *bird – birds*, *lamb – lambs*, but *sheep – sheep*.

Coastline

Genre
information

Our planet Earth is made of water and land. A coastline or beach is where the sea meets the land.

Some beaches have palm trees and golden sand, like this one. Others have steep cliffs and rocks or pebbles.

The sea is always moving. The **tide** comes in and out twice a day, changing the coastline all the time.

Lots of people go to the seaside for their holiday. Have you been to a beach? What did you see on the shore when the tide went out?

Text reproduced by permission of Hodder and Stoughton Limited

Coastline

Geography learning objectives

◆ To understand that there are different types of beach (3a).

◆ To recognise some important coastal features (3a, 3c, 4a).

◆ To recognise that people live and work at the seaside (4b, 5a).

Vocabulary

Sand, rock, cliff, shingle, dune, mud, tide, beach, shore, shells, coast, port, harbour, cove, bay, haven.

Discussing the text

◆ Introduce the text by asking the children the questions at the end: *Have you been to a beach? What did you see on the shore when the tide went out?* Encourage the children to remember as much detail as they can. What sort of activities do we take part in at the seaside? Discuss playing beach games, making sandcastles and so on.

◆ Take note of the full stops and commas when reading the text through. Make sure the children understand the difference between commas and full stops.

◆ Identify and explain any words that the children are unsure of the meaning.

◆ Point out the word *tide*. Why do the children think it is in bold? What are the other key words in the text?

◆ Brainstorm words to describe the photographs.

◆ Cover up some words in the text and encourage the children to try to predict the next words, for example *Our planet Earth is made of water and ___.*

◆ Ask the children some comprehension-style questions about the text and photographs, for example *How many times a day does the tide come in and out?*

◆ Discuss the text in terms of fiction and non-fiction. Unlike the Barnaby Bear stories in the previous chapter, this text is factual throughout. It is a purely non-fiction text.

Geography activities

◆ Encourage the children to tell you about when they have been to the seaside. Was there a sandy beach, or was it shingle, or rocky? Explain the differences. Ask them to describe the natural features of the beach in detail.

◆ Is the sand always *golden* on beaches? Compare this text with promotional literature and its use of evocative language, as in holiday brochures and tourist leaflets designed to attract people to a particular place. Let the children know that sand from coral is white and silver.

◆ Talk about what a beach is like. Is it clean? All of it? Above the tideline there can be lots of litter. Where did it come from? Why is there not usually a lot of litter below the tideline? Where does it go? Who gets it in the end? Why do the children think the beach is usually quite smooth and flat? Go on to discuss the tide and tidal processes. Some high tides are higher than others (spring tides) and others are quite low (neap tides), so some parts of the beach are 'washed clean' more often than others. How many high tides do we have daily? (Usually two, but sometimes only one as the two-tide cycle takes about 25 hours). Not all places have this pattern. Some have only one high tide per day;

unusually, some places may have three or four tides per day (for example, some places on the south coast of England).

◆ Talk about some of the main features on the coast. Where do cliffs come from? (From the landward side, they are hills. This suggests that they are hills that have been worn away.) What wore them away? Where did the rocks and soil go when they fell from the cliffs? (After falling onto the beach below, they will have been washed away by the sea and possibly some have been deposited elsewhere along the coast as sand or stones.)

◆ What jobs do people have at the seaside? (Jobs related to tourism and visits to the seaside; jobs related to the sea itself, such as the coastguard and fishing.)

◆ Where do people live near the sea? Discuss words for seaside settlements in general terms, such as *town* and *village*, then, more specifically, *port* and *harbour*. Remind the children that, just like inland, some parts of the coast are 'open country', with very little settlement.

◆ Some seaside towns have names containing the words *cove*, *bay* or *haven*. What do these words mean? Ask the children to look them up in dictionaries or encyclopedias. What do names like this tell us about places?

◆ As you are discussing the above coastal features, list them on a board or flip chart. Get the children to draw and write brief explanations about as many as they can. Or the children could draw and label a diagram showing the different parts of a beach.

Further literacy ideas

◆ Ask the children to write a story set on either a sandy beach with palm trees and golden sand or a beach with steep cliffs and rocks or pebbles. Remind the children to make sure that their stories are clearly structured.

◆ Use words from the text, for example *beach* and *meets* to revise the spellings of *ee* and *ea* words.

◆ Use the text and discussions to help create a geographical dictionary of terms. Remind the children of alphabetical order.

◆ Revise the plurals of various words in the text, for example *beaches*, *rocks*, *pebbles* and *waves*.

◆ Use non-fiction books to find out more about coastlines. Encourage the children to use the contents and index pages.

◆ Ask the children to write a sentence in answer to the last question in the text. Remind them to use commas in their lists.

Genre
illustrated
story

The Little House by the Sea

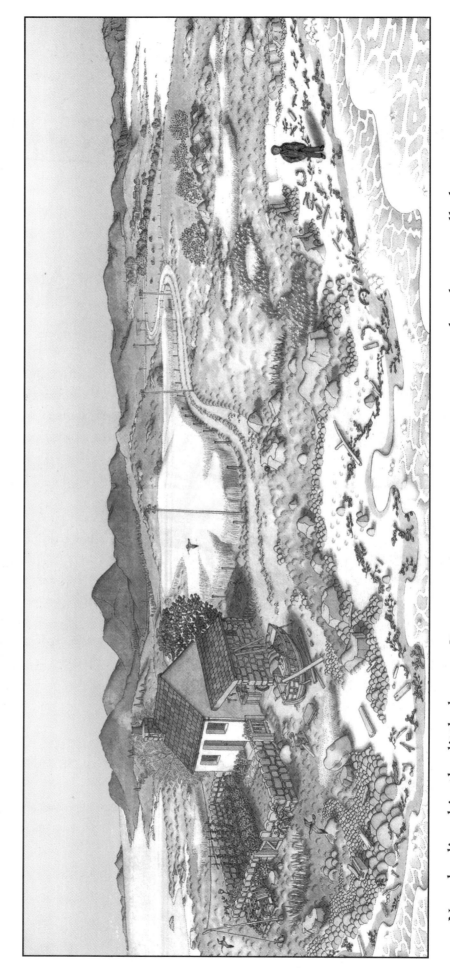

Text and illustration
© Benedict Blathwayt

Now he lived in the little house. It was neat and tidy and warm and cosy …

… but he was all alone.

The Little House by the Sea

Geography learning objectives

◆ To express their own views about places (1c).

◆ To recognise a variety of physical features (3a, 3d).

◆ To identify and describe what a place is like (3a, 6b).

◆ To recognise how places are changing and can be changed (3c, 4b, 5a).

Background notes

This story is about a man who is looking for somewhere to live. He eventually finds a place he would like to live in, but it is derelict, so he rebuilds it to make his new home.

Vocabulary

Hill, mountain, coast, rocks, field, fishing, village, valley, resort.

Discussing the text

◆ Cover the title and the picture and show the children the text. Discuss what they think the house looks like. Where do they think it is? Do they think that the fact the person in the story is *all alone* affects the setting? Why is this? Why do they think the person in the story is alone?

◆ Reveal the picture, but keep the title covered. Are the house and the setting what was expected? Talk about the details that tell us about the person in the story. Can we find anything about his hobbies, what he does each day? Use the clues in the picture, for example the boat, to start off.

◆ Talk about the phrase… *but he was all alone*. Why do the children think the man is alone? Has he always been on his own? What do they think is going to happen to him and how might the setting affect the plot of the story? There might be all sorts of explanations, and all sorts of endings to the story. The responses are limited only by the children's imaginations and the bounds of reality.

◆ Ask the children to suggest an alternative title for the story, giving reasons. Compare the children's ideas with the actual title. Do theirs give any more clues as to what the story might be about?

◆ Ask the children if they have ever been to a place like this one, and brainstorm words that would describe it. Encourage the children to think about their senses – what they would see, hear and smell.

◆ Ask the children to talk about living in this place. Would they like to live here and, if so, why? Is there anybody who would not like to live here? Why?

◆ The text says the house was *neat and tidy and warm and cosy*. What might it have been like before, when the man found it? What makes a place neat? Is *neat* the same as *tidy*, and *warm* the same as *cosy*? What are the differences? What do the children think makes a place cosy?

◆ *Neat* and *tidy* are synonyms. Can the children think of synonyms for other words in the text?

Geography activities

◆ Talk about the place. What sort of a place is it? Do the children think it might be in the UK or somewhere else? What evidence is there that it *could* be in this country?

◆ Why might the man have chosen to live here? Talk about what attracts people to different places.

◆ What features can the children see? What signs are there of people living in the area? What can be seen in the background? Children could either mark their copies of the picture, or you could cover the picture with tracing paper, and then they can mark on that the traces of human settlement, labelling what they have marked. Discuss words such as *hill* and *mountain* and possibly more locally specific words as well, such as *fell, top* and *downs*.

◆ How would this place change if lots of people came to live here to keep the man company? Do you think the man would still like to live here? Would it spoil it for the people in the village? What would it look like if it became a seaside resort?

◆ Get the children to use Post-it notes to label the features in the picture. Ask them to write a sentence or two about the attractions of the place as it is now.

◆ Ask the children to imagine they are planners who are going to build a seaside resort. They can draw an outline on tracing paper over a copy of the picture and label what they want to put on it. Ask them to write a sentence to describe the 'new' place.

◆ The man is not really *all* alone. There are signs of animal life in the picture. What animals would the children expect to find in a place like this? (Perhaps seals; fish; various sea, heath and moorland birds; deer; foxes.) Use reference books about animals of the British Isles to find out what animals might be found in a place like this.

◆ How do the children think the man would spend his day? Would he grow and catch his own food? Would he go shopping? Would it be easy for him to go shopping? How does he travel around? (There is no sign of a car or garage; he is building a boat.) Do the children think that a bus would be likely to call near this house at the end of a long lane?

Further literacy ideas

◆ Give the children the picture without the text and ask them to write a story about living in this place. This activity could be done as shared or guided writing in order to show the children how to build up the detail needed to give the reader a clear picture of the story setting.

◆ Use the figure in the story as a starting point for some work on characters. Brainstorm words that the children think would describe him. Help the children to add detail to these sentences in order to build up a detailed character sketch. As an extension activity, the children could write a similar sketch for someone who is very different to the man in this story.

◆ Use the sentence *It was neat and tidy and warm and cosy* to introduce or revise work on adjectives. Give the children different postcards or pictures of buildings or places to describe.

◆ For other work on adjectives, give the children the text with some of the words blanked out and ask them to suggest alternatives. For example, *Now he lived in the ___ house. It was ___ and tidy and ___ and cosy.* Advise the children that their words do not need to be similar to those in the text (for example, replacing *little* with *small*), but can be any words that fit the sentence.

◆ Ask the children to write a story about being *all alone*. Encourage them to think about how they would feel and to try and find words to describe these feelings. The children could be asked to write about being all alone in this particular place. Less able children might need a set of questions to help them plan their story. For example *When did you get to this place? Why did you come here? Have you always been on your own or did there used to be someone with you?*

◆ Ask the children to draw up a list of questions that they would like to ask the man in the story. They should write these questions with correct use of capital letters, full stops and question marks.

◆ Make a series of observation questions requiring the children to look carefully at the picture. For example, *How do you think the man travels around this place?* Tell the children that they must use clues in the picture to answer the questions in full, correctly punctuated sentences, including as much detail as possible. For example, *The character might be able to travel around this place in the boat when he has mended it. Until he mends the boat, he might use his bike, which is in the shed next to the house.*

Human geography

Without people there would be very little geography. A large part of geography relates to where people live and how this affects and is affected by their physical surroundings and all the activities involved in modern life, with its local and global connections. Human geography relates to the impact that people have on the land, in the widest possible sense – their economic activities and the way in which people and their settlements are linked together and interact, at all levels, from the smallest hamlet to the global community.

From an early age, children have firsthand experience of the human activities related to daily life – working, shopping, living at home, going to school, leisure activities, going to the park… Children should have the opportunity to discuss and experience various aspects of everyday life in a settlement and to consider how these activities help to shape and change the places where we live. As with physical geography, this work should begin 'at home', by looking at the human features of the children's locality and the activities that these reflect – living in a community, various aspects of work, whether it be farming or a town centre department store, a local garage or one of a row of shops in a suburban area. There may even be evidence of manufacturing in the area, perhaps on a small scale or of obtaining raw materials through quarrying, mining and so on.

The texts chosen here give opportunities to think about shopping, and the types of shop we find where, transport and its effects on the places we live in, and different types of settlement, both urban and rural, as well as a farm that attracts visitors. At least one of the types of settlement examined will probably be similar to the children's own and this familiarity can be used to develop discussion about other places included in the texts.

HUMAN GEOGRAPHY

Genre
story in the
form of
rhythmic
rhyming
couplets

Stanley Bagshaw

Stanley Bagshaw resides with his Grandma
At number 4 Prince Albert Row.

In Huddersgate (famed for its tramlines),
Up north where it's boring and slow,

Text and illustration © Bob Wilson

Stanley Bagshaw

Geography learning objectives

◆ To express their own views about a place (1c).
◆ To use geographical vocabulary (2a).
◆ To use secondary sources of information (2d).
◆ To identify and describe what places are like (3a).
◆ To recognise how places have become the way they are and how they are changing (3c).
◆ To recognise how places compare with other places (3d).

Vocabulary

Tramlines, factory, hills, washing line, dustbin, smoke, north, chimney, coal, coal fire, address, urban.

Discussing the text

◆ Cover the picture and read through the extract with the children. Ask them what they think the book is about. Do they think it is a fiction or non-fiction piece? Tell the children that there is a picture to go with the text. What sort of place do they think will be shown in the picture? What sort of place do they think Huddersgate is?

◆ Re-read the text together, emphasising the rhyme and rhythm of the words. Discuss with the children whether they think the text comes from a poem or a story. Explain that it is actually a story written in verse. Do the children know of any other stories written like this? Read some examples, such as Rupert Bear stories and Sarah Hayes's *This is the Bear,* that are written in couplets.

◆ *Up north where it's boring and slow.* Discuss this phrase with the children, explaining how the writer is being humorous, by stating a stereotype that has become established in many people's minds. Discuss humour in general. Have the children read any other poems and stories that were funny? Read some of the examples and talk about the way these poems and stories are read. Demonstrate how a reader can sometimes make a text sound funnier or more authentic by reading with an accent that is not their usual one or is exaggerated. What sort of accent do the children think a person from Huddersgate would have? Discuss accents and regional variations in speech in general.

Geography activities

◆ Examine the picture and talk about the sort of town it shows. Identify the main environmental features – factory buildings, houses in a built up area, small back yards, no garden, rows of houses. Are these new or old houses? How can we tell? How does this compare with where the children live? The children could draw their own similar or different environments and label the features.

◆ Talk about the word *tramlines*. Use some historical pictures to show what tramlines used to look like and why they were important in helping people to get to work and into the town centre. Explain that, for a long time, people did not have cars and trams were a good mode of transport. What were the disadvantages? (It was a fixed route and they were noisy.) Trams are returning to city centres to try to overcome the problems created by cars and the resulting traffic congestion. Croydon, Sheffield and Manchester, as well as many large cities abroad, are good examples of their reintroduction. Following the discussion, get the children to work in pairs to list reasons why a tram system could be a good idea in and around their nearest main town.

◆ Ask the children to imagine what it would be like to live in such a town as Huddersgate. What sort of games would they play and where? Many northern towns have cul-de-sacs dedicated as play streets as well as there being recreation grounds in the locality. How would they travel to school, shops and so on? What would the place be like at night? Would they like to live there? Why?

◆ Stanley lives at 4 Prince Albert Row. Who is it named after? Does it give us a clue about how old the houses are here? Get the children to write out their own addresses and then compare notes on what the street names say about the area. In many places, the street names may reflect old land use in, for example, the name of a farm that was once there or leafy countryside even though it is now firmly in the suburbs. Do the street names give any clues about when the street was first laid out? For example, Jubilee Road – which jubilee? Coronation Street – whose coronation?

◆ *Row* is one word for a road. Can they think of others? (*Street, crescent, close, lane, avenue* and so on.) Ask the children to list as many as they know, starting with their own type of road. This could be extended by looking for more in a local street map (or one of another place), or even by looking at a selection of pages from a local telephone directory.

◆ Huddersgate is a fictional name for a town but has its roots in Yorkshire towns such as Huddersfield and Harrogate. Look at an atlas with the children to see where Huddersfield is and how it connects to their own area. How could they travel there? Which routes could they use? Find other places on the map nearby that Stanley could visit. Could he easily get to the countryside or moors? Where would his nearest seaside place be?

◆ Show the children some pictures by industrial artists such as LS Lowry, who made paintings of urban and industrial landscapes famous. Ask them to identify some of the urban features and the elements, such as chimney smoke, which are not often seen now. Why were chimneys bad for the environment? It is possible that the children have little or no concept of a coal fire or indeed coal itself and these will need some explanation.

Further literacy ideas

◆ Can the children write a postcard to Stanley with a picture of their own area and address it correctly? Ask them to practise writing their own address first.

◆ Use the extract as a basis for a shared writing lesson. Try to add another couple of lines in a similar style. This activity could be started by brainstorming a list of words that rhyme with *slow* and *row*.

◆ Ask the children to use the picture as a basis for writing a character sketch of either Stanley or his grandmother. Advise them to include a description of what their chosen character looks like. The children will have to come up with their own ideas about the character's personality.

◆ Introduce the phrase *bird's-eye view*. Ask the children to imagine that they are either the bird on the post or the cat on the window sill and to write a description of what they see around them.

◆ In small groups or pairs, ask the children to collect books that have similar pictures of townscapes to that in the picture. Ask the children to write labels for the pictures they find, pointing out as much detail as possible, for example *drainpipe, dustbin, deckchair*.

◆ Ask the children to write a few sentences about what visitors would see if they came to visit the road where they live. With partners, ask the children to read out their description of the place and take it in turns to draw a picture using the clues read out to them. For example, *There are lots of houses in my street. Some of them have gardens with gates.*

◆ In a shared writing session, write a letter to Stanley as if he were the class pen-pal. Tell him about the locality the children live in and the sorts of things they enjoy doing. As part of the letter, ask the children to think of some questions that they would like to ask him. As an extension activity, the children could then suggest possible answers that Stanley might give.

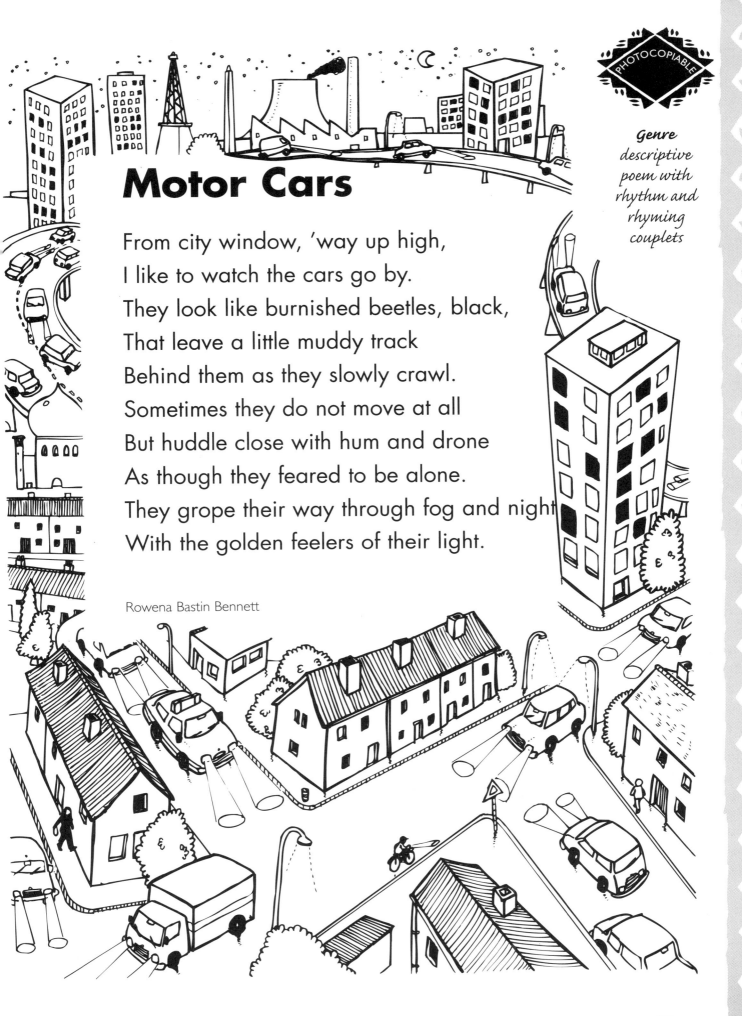

Motor Cars

Genre
descriptive
poem with
rhythm and
rhyming
couplets

From city window, 'way up high,
I like to watch the cars go by.
They look like burnished beetles, black,
That leave a little muddy track
Behind them as they slowly crawl.
Sometimes they do not move at all
But huddle close with hum and drone
As though they feared to be alone.
They grope their way through fog and night
With the golden feelers of their light.

Rowena Bastin Bennett

Motor Cars

Geography learning objectives

◆ To ask geographical questions (1a).
◆ To recognise and describe features of a place (3a, 3b).
◆ To recognise how places change (3c).
◆ To use secondary sources of information (2d).
◆ To understand how traffic affects a place (5a).

Background notes

This poem raises issues about the use of cars in towns as well as giving more opportunities to consider the features of the urban environment.

Vocabulary

Window, city, beetles, track, crawl, huddle, night, traffic, light, lorries, vans, cars.

Discussing the text

◆ Read the poem through to the children, putting emphasis on the rhyming words, such as *black* and *track*. Help the children to notice the rhythm as you read. Then read it through together.
◆ Change a whole sentence (couplet) of the poem with the children. Does it still have the same rhythm? Discuss the reasons for this, mentioning the number of syllables in the words.
◆ Discuss the unfamiliar vocabulary in the poem, such as *burnished*. Ask the children to suggest meanings for these words using the context of the poem.
◆ Talk about why the poet describes the cars as *beetles*. What does she mean when she describes their *golden feelers*? Can the children suggest any other creature that the cars could be compared to?
◆ Talk about the phrase *hum* and *drone*. What does this mean? What sounds is the writer trying to describe? Refer to the *beetles* simile and talk about all the senses referred to in the poem – the various sights and sounds.
◆ What is the *muddy track* that the cars leave behind? (The exhaust fumes.) Do the children think this is a good description?
◆ Ask the children which their favourite lines in the poem are. Is there any consensus on which part of the poem is the most popular?

Geography activities

◆ Discuss what the terms *city*, *town* and *village* mean. What are the characteristics of each? Show some pictures that indicate what each of these types of settlements looks like. A crowded city scene will help the children to make more sense of the lines in the poem.
◆ Ask the children to imagine they are looking out of the window high up above the city street. What will they see? Why do the cars look so small? Remind them of the phrase *a bird's eye view*. Why is a *beetle* a good description for a car seen in this way? What sort of building might this window be in? An office block, a block of flats? Encourage them to try to think of more imaginative places such as a clock tower, a lift or the platform of a window cleaner. Ask them to write a description of where they are and what they can see.

◆ Look at how the cars in the poem *slowly crawl*. What happens to traffic in cities? Why does it change speed? (Traffic controls, the volume of traffic, queues.) At what time of day will it be heaviest? When does the most traffic occur around school? (At the start and finish of the day.) What sort of problems occur? Can parents park easily? Take the children out into the playground and look at the area. Ask the children to note down all the different methods of controlling traffic. (For example, school signs, yellow markings outside the gates, crossing patrol.)

◆ If people didn't use their cars, how else could they travel into the city? Why do people want to go into the city? What is there in a city that attracts people? (Large shops, entertainment facilities, main offices, banks, services, housing, hospitals, museums, tourist places.) What sort of jobs will there be? Go on to relate this discussion to your local area. This could be developed into a short piece of co-operative writing on 'without our cars'.

◆ Use a map with the children to locate your nearest city or large town. Help the children to identify the communication links to it. Who has someone in their family who travels to work in a city or town? Who has been to a city centre and why? What is a city like to be in?

◆ Show some pictures of cities in other countries. What are they like? Although there are some obvious differences, try to get the children to identify the similarities such as numbers of people, amount of traffic, busy streets, buildings, shops, offices, general hustle and bustle. This could be recorded as a chart showing similarities in one column and differences in another, or you could use a variety of writing frames, for example *Traffic in ____ is different from that in ____ because ____, but it is similar in some ways because ____.*

◆ Discuss with the children other traffic issues in your local area. Every locality has its own problems – narrow roads that cause congestion or wide roads difficult to cross, noise, parking difficulties, queues, accident black spots, blind corners, bypasses and so on. Together, make a list of the ones in your area and try to identify how some of the problems are being tackled. If appropriate, walk the children round the locality and ask them to focus their observations on the traffic in the area. What are the problems and what are possible solutions?

◆ Help the children to carry out a survey of how people travel to and from school. Examine the results and ask why people choose to travel in these ways. Do most people come by car? Could more people be persuaded to walk or ride a bicycle to school? Are there enough safe routes to school to do this? What about a walking bus project?

Further literacy ideas

◆ Give the poem to small groups of children and ask them to practise reading it aloud. Allow the children time to rehearse the poem and then take it in turns to perform their readings to the class. The poem could also be read onto tape and perhaps percussion instruments included.

◆ Ask the children to make a chart with a column for each of the groups of words that rhyme, for example *night* and *light*; *black* and *track*. Tell the children to think of as many other words as possible to add to each column.

◆ In a guided writing lesson, use the phrase *burnished beetles* to introduce the children to the idea of alliteration. Give the children a list of animals to try to describe in a similar way, for example *crawling caterpillar*, *slithering snake*. The children could then use these animals in a poem written in a shared writing lesson.

◆ Ask the children to use the opening phrase – *From city window*, as the starting point for a story.

◆ Ask the children to choose a mode of transport and then write a 'what am I?' style poem. Tell the children to put in as much detail as possible, but not the name of the transport, so that the reader can build up a really clear picture in his or her head.

Genre
speech-based
story giving
information

Packed Lunch for the Castle

You can see for miles. Can we walk around the wall?

Some of it. Some parts are not safe.

Steve Eales (text) and Rachel and Chris Mendes (illustration)

Packed Lunch for the Castle

Geography learning objectives

◆ To express their views about a place (1c).

◆ To relate fieldwork skills to the classroom (1b, 2b, 7b).

◆ To identify and describe what places are like (3a).

◆ To recognise how places have become the way they are and how they are changing (3c).

◆ To make observations about features in the environment (4a).

Background notes

This text offers a good opportunity to explore some strong geographical work from a historical topic, and gives balance to the location and context of a castle, both past and present.

Vocabulary

Castle, wall, miles, buildings, ruins, keep, tower, turrets, ramparts, gateway, village, church, field, town, features.

Discussing the text

◆ Encourage the children to tell you about what they can see happening in the picture. What are the different figures doing in and around the castle grounds? Talk about who the figures might be, for example a school party, a family, people working at the castle.

◆ Why do the children think some of the figures are visiting the castle? How might they have travelled to it? How long will they stay? What will they do while they are there?

◆ Talk about the setting of the castle, and see if the children can tell you what is behind the castle. What sort of a place is this? (It is probably a village with countryside behind, but it could be the edge of a larger town, but make the point that we cannot tell for certain from the picture.)

◆ Have any of the children visited a castle? Where was it? Ask the children to describe the buildings they saw. Were the buildings more or less complete or mostly in ruins? Discuss why any building might come to be ruined.

◆ Ask the children what time of year they think the story is set in. Are there any clues, for example falling leaves? Can they make a guess at what the weather is like?

◆ Read and discuss the extract and talk about the punctuation and the importance of context in making sense of the sentences.

◆ Who do the children think is 'speaking' the text – from whose point of view was it written? (A teacher and the class going around the castle on a visit.) Role-play the text with different children taking the parts. Can they improvise a continuation of the conversation?

Geography activities

◆ Focus on the class in the picture being taken around the castle by their teacher. What will the children see and do? Perhaps look at the castle, walk the walls, look at the view, sketch a landscape or take some measurements. Relate this, if possible, to an out-of-classroom visit the children have made themselves and the sort of activities they will have experienced. It is an opportunity to use the geographical and historical aspects of the curriculum together to give a balanced approach to a visit.

◆ Ask the children to identify all the features they can see – the different types of buildings and landscape elements. On a flip chart, using two headings – *natural* and *human*, complete two lists of the features, asking the children to work out which column each should be placed in. If the children are able, an interesting debate could be had on the word *field*, which is both a natural and man-made feature. Can they think of any others? (For example, orchards and gardens.)

◆ The picture lends itself to discussion about the weather. What are the clues about the weather and the possible season? It would be appropriate to revise the names and characteristics of the four seasons and the months of the year. The children could be asked to consider their responses, discuss with partners and then give reasons for their answers. (For example, no shadows, no evidence of puddles, leaves falling from the trees, people wearing light coats and so on.) An extension question could be *How does the weather influence our choice of clothes?*

◆ Talk about the residential area in the background of the picture. What can the children see there? Can they make out any types of houses and other features that stand out? Remind them of the house types such as flats, detached, semi-detached, terraced, and have pictures of these available if possible. Discuss the types of houses the children live in, referring to the pictures if necessary. On a wider scale, ask the children what the differences are between a town and a village. Which do the children live in? Ask the children to write a description of their settlement, giving details of what makes it a town or village and so on. If they have a good understanding about a basic settlement, it might be a good time to introduce the notion of suburbs where much of the population lives.

◆ Ask the children to imagine what the place would have looked like long ago, when there were people living in the castle. Who would have lived there? Would there have been a village then and if so, what would it have looked like? Ask the children to draw two pictures, perhaps of somewhere in the local area – one showing life long ago, perhaps in the Middle Ages and the other, life today. First discuss what would not have been available – cars, street lights, tarmac roads, modern clothing and so on. Share some pictures of such a time and ask the children to identify which features from the past are similar to those we have now. (For example, roads would have been tracks, houses would have been made of different material, transport would have been carts instead of cars, and there are many other things that would have been there in essentially the same form, such as the castle, the church (although perhaps smaller), some houses (but not the same ones). Would there have been a market place, or a village green, perhaps?

◆ Why are some parts of the castle walls not safe? Why have they got like that? Discuss with the children how buildings that have been damaged or left uncared for decay and become unsafe. Talk about the safety aspects of going into unknown buildings. Stress that even new buildings can be unsafe because there may be unfinished work inside.

◆ Look at a labelled diagram of another castle, detailing the keep, wards, tower, ramparts, turrets and so on. Then relate this to the picture, asking the children to locate which bits of the castle they can see. Go on to ask: *Why are the windows so small, why was a lookout necessary and why was being able to see for miles so important?* An extension question could be: *Why was the well inside the castle grounds?*

◆ Ask the children to label as many important aspects as they can see, both of the castle and the landscape. This is an opportunity to discuss the layout of the castle and find the entrance gate, lookout tower, courtyard, well and keep.

Further literacy ideas

◆ Use the question asked in the extract to reinforce the children's understanding of the difference between statements and questions. Ask the children to write a list of questions about the text. Then see if they can turn these questions into statements. Differentiate this activity by asking the children to write questions for specific figures in the picture. For example, what questions might the schoolchildren ask and how would these questions be different to the questions a visitor from abroad might ask? For example, the children might ask about how the castle was defended, or if it was ever attacked. Visitors from other places might want to know why it was built here, and who lived here.

◆ Use the text to initiate work on sentences. What does a sentence need for it to make sense? Ask the children to write sentences about the picture, describing what is happening, what the castle is like, what can be seen from the castle and so on.

◆ Write a short story together, possibly over a couple of days, about *A Visit to the Castle*. Brainstorm a list of questions that the children will need to answer, for example about who was visiting the castle, why they were visiting and what they did when they were there.

◆ Ask the children to choose a character from the picture to write about. Advise them to make up a home for the person (perhaps, but not necessarily, in the village), a reason for him or her visiting the castle and how he or she travelled there.

◆ Give the children an enlarged copy of the picture and ask them to write labels and captions for it, describing activities for a visitor to enjoy at the castle.

◆ Brainstorm a list of adjectives to describe the castle. You could use other pictures of castles to help the children add to their word list.

◆ Give the children the topic *Castle Characters* and ask them to write about different characters who would have lived in a castle, for example, the lord/owner of the castle and his family, their followers (soldiers), servants (What servants would there be? How many would be needed?), someone to look after horses, a blacksmith for looking after the arms as well as shoeing horses. Advise them to include 'good' and 'bad' characters.

◆ *Some parts are not safe.* Use this sentence to investigate the difference between positive and negative statements. Brainstorm words and phrases that are negative or positive, for example *not, no, can't, won't, do not.*

◆ Use the text to introduce the idea of tense. Ask the children to write out the text as if it had happened already, that is in the past tense. Investigate what happens to the words when they are written this way, for example changing *can* to *could*.

Genre
*narrative
fiction*

When We Went
to the Park

When Grandpa and I put on our coats

and went to the park …

We saw …

Text and illustration © Shirley Hughes

When We Went to the Park

Geography learning objectives
◆ To predict features in a particular place (1c).
◆ To identify and use geographical vocabulary (2a).
◆ To recall and recognise features in a park (3a, 6a).
◆ To recognise that places change over time (3c, 4b, 5a).

Background notes
This is an open-ended extract that gives the children plenty of opportunities to predict what will be seen in a certain place. It encourages them to think not only about the features of a park, but also what and who you might meet with there.

Vocabulary
Park, flowers, trees, swings, space, sandpit, lake, pond, river, bridge, footpath, seat.

Discussing the text
◆ Show the children the picture and ask them to describe what they see. Put a list of words suggested by the children on the board, for example *baby*, *old man*, *child*. Ask the children to predict who they think the characters in the story are. Do they think they are related? What do they think is happening in the story? Where do they think the girl and the man are going? Write up the children's suggestions of places.

◆ Reveal the text to the children and read it through together. Compare the text of the story with the children's previous suggestions. The only character actually named in the extract is Grandpa, but ask the children if they can work out who all the other characters in the picture are just from what they can see. Who is the narrator, the *I* of the story?

◆ Talk about why the characters might be going to the park. Do the children think this story is set in a quiet place or a busy town? Draw their attention to the buildings in the background of the picture if they have not already noticed them.

◆ What do the children think the child and her grandfather are going to do in the park? What would they see? Talk about any trips the children have made to a park. What did they see? What did they do? What do parks have?

◆ Discuss what time of year the children think this story might be taking place. Can they find any clues in the pictures or the text? (Draw attention to the clothing.)

Geography activities
◆ Discuss with the children what they understand by a park. Why was the little girl going there? Why did she need her coat on? Ask them to list what sort of things she might enjoy in the park. (Include the features such as flowers, grass, lake, ducks, plus playground equipment.) If they have time, they could draw the objects next to their lists.

◆ Ask the children about the parks in your local area. Are there parks, playgrounds, open spaces or recreation grounds? What are they like? Who goes there, how often and how do they travel there?

What do the children like doing best? Ask them to write a brief account of their favourite thing to do in a park, how often they are able to do it and how they get to the park.

◆ Are there any notices in parks? What do they ask us to do and not to do? Why are these rules necessary? Brainstorm a list of park safety rules and where the notices would best be placed.

◆ What is the best weather to visit a park? How will the park change over the seasons? This is a good opportunity to revise seasonal weather variations and the sort of changes they bring to the landscape, and to people both inside houses and outside. The children could draw pictures of a park in all four seasons and some could also write about the changes. Remind the children of the child and her grandfather putting on their coats and get them to think about what sort of clothes are best in the different seasons.

◆ Which other places are good to visit to play? (Woodlands, the seaside, countryside and so on.) What sort of things can they do in each of the different places? Do they need special clothes or equipment? You could develop this into a group activity where, after brainstorming places to play, you allocate one place to each group who then discuss and note down what it has to offer, if it is suitable for all weathers and so on.

◆ Take the children out into the playground and discuss the play areas there. What else would they like to see? Suggest some patterns that could be painted onto the playground and ask the children to make up some games to go with them. Back in the classroom, ask groups of children to design a new playground for the school. When they have finished, discuss their suggestions and come to a class decision on the best ideas and designs. The children could then present them to the staff and school, perhaps in an assembly.

Further literacy ideas

◆ Ask the children to list everything the two characters might have seen when they went to the park. Advise them to choose one of these things, for example a duck pond or a play park, and ask them to draw and label it.

◆ Give the children some comprehension questions about the picture and text. For example, *What did the little girl do before she went the park?* Encourage the children to write their answers in full sentences. More able children may be able to come up with their own questions about the picture and swap these with partners to answer.

◆ Tell the children to choose one of the characters in the story and draw a labelled picture of them. Advise them to put in small details like the colour of hair and eyes. They could also label the clothes they are wearing, including colour words. More able children could write some fuller sentences about their character.

◆ As part of a shared writing lesson, help the children to write a short story about a similar visit to a park.

◆ Use some of the words in the story as the basis for a word-sum exercise. For example, $p+u+t = put; t+h+e = the$.

◆ Ask the children to write down some of the things that they think the woman in the picture is saying to Grandpa and the little girl as they go off to the park. For example, *Be careful. Stay near your Grandpa.* This text could be put into speech bubbles.

◆ Give the children a starting point similar to that in the story, but with a different place as the setting. For example, *We went to the zoo… We went to the shops…* Ask the children to write a list for each place, starting with the words *I saw*, and get some of the children to read their lists out loud to the other children in the class. This could be turned into a game where each child in a group has to add something to the list of things seen.

Shopping

Genre
report with
illustrations

- Sam's dad buys his newspaper at the local corner shop on his way to work.
- Sam and his sister go to the local shopping parade to buy fresh bread after having a haircut.
- Sam's new school uniform comes from the department store in the centre of town.
- Every week, Sam and his family go to do their food shopping at the superstore on the edge of town.

Shopping

Geography learning objectives

◆ To recognise that there are different types of shop (3a, 6a).

◆ To understand that different shops serve different needs (3c).

◆ To recognise how places compare with other places (3d).

◆ To make observations about where things are located (4a).

Vocabulary

Local shop, corner shop, parade, supermarket, superstore, department store, grocer, greengrocer, market.

Discussing the text

◆ Show the children the pictures without the text and ask the children what they can see. Talk about the shops around the area where the children live. Which picture is similar to the children's own area? Which is the most different?

◆ Why do the children think people would go to each of the shops shown in the picture? What sorts of things would people buy and who would go there?

◆ Read through each of the points with the children. Discuss the term *local* that is used twice. What do the children understand by this term? Ask them to define to you what they consider to be their local area.

◆ Discuss the phrase *Open till late* that is displayed on the local corner shop. Talk about whether or not this is a full sentence. Redefine with the children what a sentence is and what it must consist of in order to be classed as a sentence.

◆ Go through the different purchases and services Sam and his family buy and use, and where they go for them. For each item, ask the children where they go.

Geography activities

◆ Ask the children if they have any shops near where they live. What sort of shop is it? Is it a single shop, or part of a parade? Where do they go to shop for small, everyday things? What would their families need to buy from a big shop?

◆ Give the children a list of things to buy and ask them to identify where in their area they would go to make their purchases. Write the responses up on a flip chart for reference.

◆ Visit the shops in your local area. If possible, ask the shopkeepers if the children can ask them questions. Before the visit, establish the sort of thing the children want to find out about, for example opening times, number of people working there, deliveries, how does the shop owner know when more supplies are needed. Using the information, the children can write a report of their visit.

◆ Talk to the children about their local supermarket or superstore. Have they been there? How often does the family visit? If a visit is possible, get the children to identify all the typical components of the outside area. These will probably include a large car park, trolley parks, any other facilities such as cashpoints, bottle banks and so on. Why do people visit supermarkets if they can buy all the things at specialist shops? Having identified the advantages of the supermarket, create a questionnaire including them, such as easy parking; goods under one roof; large choice of goods; other facilities;

coffee shop; late opening hours; easy access; cheaper prices. When the questionnaire has been agreed on, let the children interview some adults and ask them to rank these aspects in order of importance. The results can then be fed into a simple database and processed. Children can discuss their findings. What are the most usual reasons people give for using a supermarket? Are these the reasons the children would have expected?

◆ Have any of the children been to a market, perhaps an open-air one? Show the children pictures of shops and markets around the world. Try to include some unusual ones such as floating markets in Thailand and Amsterdam or trading stores in Canada. What information can the children obtain from the pictures? Can they tell anything about the climate or the life people lead? Help the children to use an atlas to identify where some of the places are. Where are they in relation to this country?

◆ Set up a role-play with some shops in the classroom. Ask the children to consider what they will sell. How will they work out how much to charge for the goods? How will they get the goods? Suggest that they include delivery people in their characters. From this, go on to talk about what sort of things the children had delivered to the shop and where this produce would come from. Do they know where bananas and pineapples come from, for example?

◆ Discuss other methods of shopping with the children, for example from catalogues, by telephone, the Internet, at car boot sales. Access an Internet shopping site and show the children how it works. Discuss why some people may prefer to shop in this way. What are the advantages and disadvantages? Does the local superstore have an Internet shopping service? How does it work?

Further literacy ideas

◆ Separate the four sections of the text from the pictures and ask the children to match them. An extension activity could be to give the children each of the pictures and ask them to write a few sentences or even a paragraph to accompany the illustration. Less able children could be asked to provide labels and captions for the pictures.

◆ Use the text to introduce the children to or revise the use of possessive apostrophes, for example *Sam's*.

◆ Ask the children to write a shopping list for each store shown in the pictures. Then help them to run their lists on, separating with commas.

◆ Together, make a web diagram with Sam's name in the middle and all the information you have found out about him around the outside. For example, Sam has a sister; he goes to a school where the children wear uniform.

◆ Use the word *parade* to start an investigation into words that are spelled the same but have different meanings, for example *cricket*, *scale*.

◆ Choose one of the pictures and ask the children to write an advertisement for the local paper, explaining what items can be bought in this particular place.

◆ Tell the children to imagine they go to one of the shops shown in the pictures and to write a short story about their visit. Explain that during their visit, they bump into Sam and his family. Advise them to use information from the text to include in their story. Perhaps Sam was with his mum buying his new school uniform. He tried on a new white shirt but the sleeves were too long.

◆ Look at the bulleted sentences. Why do the children think the bullets have been used? (Each makes a separate point – the bullet emphasises this fact; they are used for impact.) Use each of the sentences as a story starter or as a sentence that must be included at some point in a story.

Genre
visitor's leaflet, advertisement

Cannon Hall

OPEN FARM

Animal Magic

As seen on T.V

YORKSHIRE TOURIST BOARD
White Rose Awards
for Tourism
2000
FINALIST

The Perfect Family *Day Out*

Admission Charges

Adults: £2.25
Children & O.A.P.s: £1.75

Parties of 20 or more visitors all pay the child rate. (Adults and children) Party rate includes readmission on the day and a full guided tour.
Under 3s are FREE.

Opening Hours

Summer – (April to September)
10.30 – 4.30 Every day
Winter – (October to March)
10.30 – 4.00 Every day
Open every day except – Christmas Day

We regret that dogs (except Guide Dogs) are not allowed inside the farm. We reserve the right to withdraw any attraction without notice.

The Award Winning

Cannon Hall

OPEN FARM

Cannon Hall Farm, Cawthorne, Barnsley, South Yorkshire S75 4AT
Tel: 01226 790427 Fax: 01226 792511
Email: cannonhallfarm@btconnect.com
www.cannonhallfarm.co.uk

How to find us

You will find us directly behind Cannon Hall Museum, Cannon Hall Country Park, Cawthorne

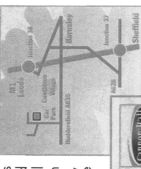

About five miles west of Barnsley. Set in the beautiful rolling foothills yet within sight of the M1 motorway.

Car Park

You'll find ample space available in our new Car/Coach Park. Tastefully landscaped as part of a much larger scheme designed to regenerate the traditional parkland landscape in which the farm is set. Parking £1 up to four hours, £1.50 over four hours. Coaches free.

Based on an original design by Storm Design

Cannon Hall
OPEN FARM

Key
1 Farm Entrance
2 Tearoom
3 Farmshop
4 New Car Park
5 Disabled Car Parking
6 Adventure Playground
7 Pigs & Piglets
8 Goats & Kids
9 Small Animals
10 Indoor Picnic Area for Schools
11 Chick Hatchery

Baby Animals appear almost every day. Lambs and Goat kids in the spring. Donkey and Pony foals in the summer and Calves, Piglets, Chickens, Guinea Pigs and Rabbits all year round. You'll always find new faces whenever you visit. Animal food is available for a small fee. You can feed Goats, Sheep, Ponies, Donkeys, Cattle and Llamas.

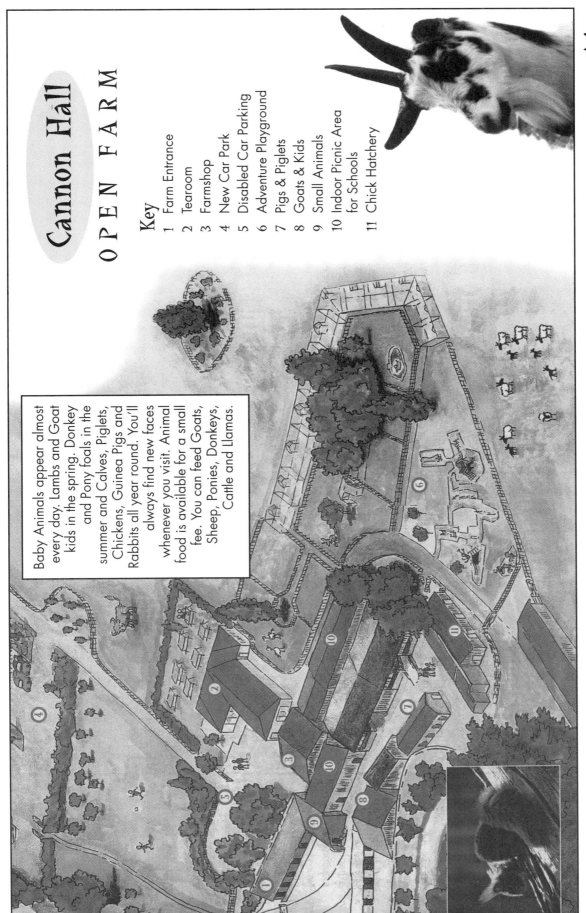

Based on an original design by Storm Design

Cannon Hall Open Farm

Geography learning objectives

◆ To express views about places (1c).

◆ To use a map or aerial view plan (2c).

◆ To make maps and plans (2e).

◆ To make observations about where things are located (4a).

◆ To recognise how places have become the way they are and how they change (3c, 3e, 4b, 5a).

Background notes

Farms today often have to diversify in order to make a profit. Many of them have become 'pick your own' farms, with additional facilities for visitors, some become more like garden centres, while others develop an informational/educational role. The latter is the route that Cannon Hall Farm has taken. Examination of it raises issues about farming and change in the modern world.

Many attractions produce leaflets or brochures similar to this one and these can provide a helpful basis to develop a range of geographical skills and understanding within a local context.

Vocabulary

Brochure, animal, farm, chicken, rabbit, llama, admission, opening hours, magic, buildings, picnic, address, regenerate, arable.

Discussing the text

◆ Show the text to the children to introduce it, perhaps even folding the first page into its three sections to look more like a leaflet. Establish with the children what the text is – a brochure or leaflet, then go through what each different part of the information tells us (and that the largest section is a map and so on). What is the aim of this text? How would the reader use it?

◆ Go through the different information in more detail and the way the different sections are laid out. Ask the children why different parts of the text are written in different fonts. What is the effect of this on the reader? Discuss how the text is very different from a story. Draw out understanding that it is in sections with headings, there is no narrative, not all of the sentences are complete, there is little or no punctuation in some parts, it is giving information and trying to persuade the reader.

◆ Talk about the abbreviation O.A.P.s under Admission Charges. Do the children know what these letters stand for and why the words are not written out in full?

◆ Some of the information is in brackets, for example (Adults and Children). Why do the children think this is? It is, for instance, used to give extra or supplementary information, to clarify what has been stated before.

◆ Look at the website address. Talk about web addresses in general and how they are different from postal addresses. Show the children a few more web addresses and identify any common characteristics, for example the co.uk or com suffixes. Follow this work up by comparing the farm's e-mail address with its postal address. Talk about the different elements of a postal address and the importance of including the postcode.

◆ Read through the different elements of the text in more detail, possibly over two or three days, and make sure the children understand the vocabulary. What does *tastefully landscaped* mean? Help the children to appreciate that this wording is part of the persuasive nature of the text.

Geography activities

◆ Establish what the children already know of or expect from farms. What do they expect a farm to have? How is this farm different? What does it have that they would not expect to find on a traditional, working farm? What are the clues on the map alone that visitors are expected? Ask the children to use the page with the map to make compare-and-contrast notes on this farm and a 'normal' farm, under headings such as *Animals, Buildings, Land areas, Parking facilities*.

◆ Ask the children to plan a day out to the farm for themselves and their family. Let them know they will need to work out the best time and season to go, how much they will need to pay and what they want to see, and whether they will buy lunch or take a picnic. This could be extended by discussing with the children how to plan a route around the farm once they are there. Where will they start? What would they like to include? Get them to make notes for the route they will take and what they will see at each major point.

◆ With a big map or road atlas, locate Cannon Hall Farm, using the road maps and information provided on the first page. Where is it near? Help the children to work out the journey there from school or their home, travelling by car.

◆ Using school resource books and information on the leaflet, ask the children to draw labelled pictures of the animals and birds they would see on a visit to the farm. Start by identifying the animals they can find on the brochure – in both the text and pictures – and finding out as much as they can about them. Discuss whether they might see other animals as well. Do they think this might change as the seasons change? Get the children to extend their list as a result and to find out about the additions to the list.

◆ Talk to the children about different types of farm – arable, sheep, cattle, mixed, fruit, for example. Are there any farms near you? Is a visit possible? It is important to introduce children to the concept that farms are businesses and as such have inputs and outputs – for example, food is given to cows which produce milk and meat; seeds are sown, given fertiliser and water and crops are harvested.

◆ Discuss with children where milk comes from. Today, the family is just as likely to buy it in the supermarket as have it delivered. Many children are unaware of the origins of a bottle of milk. This is a good opportunity to trace the milk back to the cow and produce a flow chart from grass to milk bottle or carton. The same idea can be used to trace the path from wheat to bread.

◆ As a whole class, use a floor playmat that shows either a countryside or farm layout. Mediate as the children discuss where to position a range of machinery, animals and buildings for a farm. What sort of farm will they want it to be – animals, arable, mixed? Then ask the children to draw a picture or plan of their farm, labelling the main features.

◆ Use an OS map or aerial photograph to let the children identify a farm settlement. What elements belonging to the farm can they see? (For example, fields; farm buildings, such as barns and the farmhouse; perhaps a stream.) Does it seem near or far to other settlements? Does it have farm roads or tracks?

Further literacy ideas

◆ Ask the children to highlight all the words and phrases that are meant to persuade someone to visit the farm – for example *As seen on T.V*, *Perfect*, *Award Winning*. This might be best done as a guided reading session to ensure that the children fully understand the terminology.

◆ Re-read the postal address on the leaflet, then ask the children to help you to rewrite it as you would on an envelope – on separate lines and without the commas. Remind them that certain words have capital letters. Can they tell you which? Then ask the children to write out their own and the school's address correctly. Use this as an introduction to letter-writing. Revise the layout of a simple letter, showing the children where to put the address. Can they remember how to start and end a letter? A follow-up activity could involve asking the children to write to the farm as if they were a parent or teacher wanting to take a family or school party. Ask the children to think of a question that they could ask in their letter. For example, suggest to the children that one of the party is disabled and that they need to find out about disabled access to and around the farm. Alternatively, the children could imagine that they have recently visited the farm and are writing to thank the owners and to comment on what they saw on their trip.

◆ Compare and contrast the format, styles and wording of e-mail and postal addresses. Give the children a selection of postal addresses and the corresponding e-mail addresses. Can the children match one with the other, identifying any elements that are similar?

◆ Give the children a copy of just the *How to find us* section and ask them to write a list of instructions on how to get to the farm. Start by discussing instructions with the children and how to write them – simple, straightforward, only one step at a time, must be in the right order, use vocabulary such as *First* and *Then*, make sure everything is included and so on. For children who find this difficult, they could write out instructions in the same way for getting from one place to another on the farm (see the geography activities).

◆ Use the text as a starting point for looking at nouns for animal young, for example *sheep – lamb*; *goat – kid*; *cow – calf* and so on. What about *pony* and *foal*?

◆ Investigate collective nouns, for example a *herd* of cattle, a *flock* of sheep.

◆ From the text, revise or introduce work on spelling regular and irregular plurals, for example *pony – ponies, calf – calves* and so on.

◆ If the children have made drawings and plans for their own farm, ask them to imagine they are going to open the farm to visitors and need to create a leaflet to advertise it and give information. Let them use ICT to practise using different fonts and text sizes to create an outline of the front of their own leaflet. Remind them it should be clear and attractive to potential visitors.

Our town

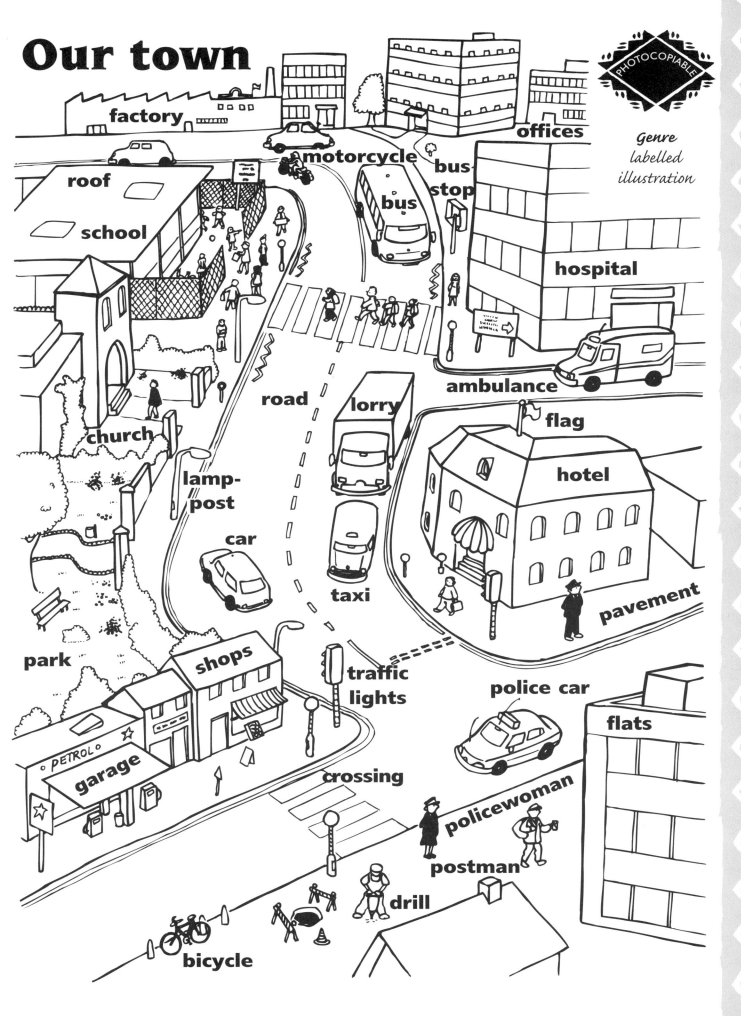

Genre
labelled
illustration

PHOTOCOPIABLE

Our town

Geography learning objectives

◆ To use geographical vocabulary (2a).

◆ To recognise features of their town (3a, 6a).

◆ To describe and compare different places (3d).

◆ To understand that people do jobs in different places (4b).

Background notes

This piece is suitable for using with younger children as it introduces a picture of an urban area that allows for extensive use and practice of vocabulary, together with simple themes such as occupations.

Vocabulary

Office, pavement, church, hotel, ambulance, vehicle, motorcycle, traffic lights, taxi, bicycle, lorry, crossing, bus, road, hospital, factory, flat, roof, garage, shop, bus stop, park, services.

Discussing the text

◆ Look at what a 'town' is. How does the picture show us it is a town? How does it compare with our town or the nearest town? What sorts of things do we find in towns?

◆ Read the captions aloud together. Check the pronunciation of more difficult words like *ambulance*.

◆ Show the children the picture with some of the captions covered up. Ask the children to suggest possible captions and then compare them with those used by the author.

◆ Discuss some of the figures in the picture. Ask the children what the different people might be saying and why they are in the town.

◆ Talk about any trips that the children have made to a town. Did they see any buildings of the types that are in the picture? What other buildings did the children see?

Geography activities

◆ Discuss with the children what sort of environment this is. Look at the vocabulary and see if the children notice that these are all human features. Ask them to think of some physical features that might be around the town, such as a lake, hills or a river.

◆ How does this place compare to where the children live? Discuss the constituents of their own area and then ask them to draw a large picture in the same style, labelling the features in the same way. This could be repeated as a floor exercise, with a group of children putting the features onto a floor map by using Lego or similar blocks.

◆ The picture lends itself to talking about position words, relating to early map work. For example, *the postman is <u>next to</u> the pram*, *the ambulance is <u>in front of</u> the hospital*. This can be reinforced in a practical way at the end of a PE lesson when the children are standing in a line. Ask children in turn to go and stand, behind, in front of, next to, to the left of a person and so on.

◆ On a flip chart, make a list of the buildings in the picture and ask the children to work out the jobs that people might do in these places. The children could also identify the people who help us and provide services. Who has been to a hospital? What about a hotel? Where would we go to get petrol …to play …to learn …to buy something?

◆ Talk about the various things that are going on in the streets. Which types of vehicle are there? How do people cross the road safely? How does this compare with our streets around our homes and school? How do we cross the road? Ask the children to tell you what they know about the Green Cross Code.

◆ Ask the children to give directions from one place on the picture to another. You may need to revise basic directions such as *turn right, left, go straight on, turn the corner*. Advise the children to try giving directions to each other – first to places in the classroom and then round the school. Is this an easy thing to do? Why not? (We know the route in our heads, but it is often difficult to put it clearly into words.)

◆ Together, make a large collage of the scene for display, with labels of all the features and people.

◆ Look at some of LS Lowry's works, of industrial scenes with matchstick-type figures. Give a different one to each group if you can and ask the children to study the painting and then create their own pictures in Lowry style.

Further literacy ideas

◆ Ask the children to choose a figure in the picture. Ask them to write a few sentences about why he or she is in the town and what he or she is doing. Discuss tenses and ask the children to rewrite sentences as if it had happened in the past and as if it was going to happen in the future

◆ Give the children a copy of the picture without the labels and ask them to label the buildings, vehicles and other important elements.

◆ Ask the children to make a list of all the compound words in the picture, for example *postman, motorcycle*. Beside this list, ask the children to write down all the labels that consist of two smaller words, but that are not joined together, for example *police car, traffic light*.

◆ Ask the children to write down what they think one or more of the characters in the picture is saying. Help them to use speech marks correctly. More able children could write a conversation between two of the characters.

◆ Look at simple prefixes like *bi* in *bicycle*. Do the children know what a cycle with three wheels is called? Can the children think of other words that have prefixes? Are there any with different prefixes but the same root, such as *bicycle, tricycle, unicycle, inside, outside*, or any which use the same prefix, for example *triangle, tricycle, tripod; telephone, television, telescope*?

◆ Use words in the text to introduce or revise homophones with the children. For example, *our – hour; road – rode*.

◆ Use the text to investigate adding *ing* to certain words, for example *crossing, shopping, parking*. Get the children to write sentences using the new words they have made ending in *-ing* and encourage them to talk about how they have been used, for example as an adjective in *shopping arcade* or a noun in *Parking prohibited*.

Bella's Big Adventure

Genre
*story in a
familiar setting*

TEACHING WITH TEXT GEOGRAPHY ages 5–7

SCHOLASTIC

HUMAN GEOGRAPHY

Text and illustration © Benedict Blathwayt

The river grew wider

TEACHERS'
NOTES

Bella's Big Adventure

Geography learning objectives

◆ To use geographical vocabulary (2a).

◆ To make comparisons between places (3d).

◆ To recognise that places can, and do, change over time (5a).

Vocabulary

Landscape, bridge, boat, barge, canoe, scarecrow, village, church, fields, fisherman, train, campsite, river, bank, meander, source, transport.

Discussing the text

◆ Look at the picture. What does it show? Introduce the word *landscape*. Explain that this picture is from a book called *Bella's Big Adventure*. Who do the children think Bella might be? (Bella is the goose in the foreground, swimming down the river.)

◆ Talk about what the children can see in the picture, encouraging them to pick out details. Have the children ever been anywhere like this? When was it? What did they do when they were there?

◆ Talk about any health and safety points that are raised by the picture, for example swimming in rivers, playing on or near railway lines.

◆ After shared reading of the extract, create a story planner as a class, using suggestions from the children as to what might have happened in the story so far and/or what might happen next. Does the phrase *The river grew wider* give any indication? What does it imply? Talk specifically about the setting and how this might influence how the story progresses. Identify Bella and talk about how one or more of the other characters in the picture might be involved in the story. Since the essence of this is using the imagination, it is not necessary to have the book – there is no 'right' answer to this. Encourage the children to think about different ways in which the story might develop.

◆ Talk about how the same characters and story would be influenced if the setting were different. How would Bella be affected if the weather changed or if she were on a narrow, twisty river?

◆ Look at each of the people in the picture. What are they doing and why do the children think they are here?

Geography activities

◆ What type of place does the picture show? Is it countryside or town? What sort of settlement can the children see? Can they tell what season it is? How? What clues are there? (Look at the trees and their leaves, the activities of the people in the picture and so on.) Ask them to write a sentence stating the time of year of the story and list all the clues that helped them come to that decision.

◆ Discuss the course of the river. What river features can they see? (River banks, bends – meanders, reed beds.) How does the river change? What does the sentence *The river grew wider* tell us about the river before this point? Ask the children to examine the picture and compare the width of the river where the rowing boat is to that where Bella is. Talk about which way a river flows – from the source to the sea or lake and so on.

◆ Look at the many ways in which the river is being used. Ask the children to write brief descriptions of these uses. Help them to add to this how the land on either side is used. (For example, for farming, road and rail communications, settlement, woodland.) Why are there no buildings close to the river? Encourage the children to consider what happens when it has been very wet and the river is high.

◆ Ask the children to list the different types of transport in the picture. What are the different ways in which places are connected? (Railway, river, roads, cycle paths, footpaths.) Look at the way sheep are moved from field to field. Why, in this place, would this be a relatively safe way of moving them? (Lack of traffic, the gate is closed, there is a dog to help shepherd them.)

◆ Discuss the difference between work and recreation activities. Ask the children to note down the jobs they can find in the picture, then list the ways the area is being used for recreation. Tell them to write a statement on what makes this an interesting place for people to visit.

◆ Ask the children to find the main farm buildings (in the top right of the picture). What sort of farming activities can they see? (Raising cows, sheep farming, growing corn, harvesting hay and so on.) Talk about the 'hidden' income. For example, the campsite is probably owned by the farmer and so he would earn fees from the site; perhaps also some fishing fees.

◆ Look at the settlement. What sorts of buildings and services can they see? (Residential buildings, church, railway station). What will people not be able to buy here? How could people travel to town for shopping? Why would there be so few shops and services in this place?

◆ How does this place compare with where the children live? What are the main similarities and differences between the places? Ask the children to work with partners to list the similarities and differences on a large sheet of paper. Then get together to share all the findings with the class.

◆ Ask the children to examine the picture to identify the things they think would change most over time (for example 25 years). What do they think this place would look like in 50 years, or 100 years? Would the river grow wider still?

Further literacy ideas

◆ Ask the children to select one of the characters in the picture and write about what they can see from this person's point of view, for example the fisherman sitting in the field with the cows who will see Bella as she canoes past him. Alternatively, the children could write from the point of view of one of the animals in the picture.

◆ Tell the children you want them to label the picture. First, brainstorm nouns and adjectives for the picture, for example *black birds, tall trees, wide river, happy children, white duck*.

◆ Investigate how the spelling and pronunciation of verbs changes according to the tense that they are written in for example *grow – growing – grew*. Make a list of verbs from the picture, such as *rowed, was walking, fishes, swims* and get the children to change the tense of these words.

◆ Re-read the extract to introduce the children to comparative adjectives like *wide – wider – widest*. Together, use words you have noted in discussing the picture as a starting point for making lists of similar words. For example, the tree: *tall – taller – tallest*; the train: *long – longer – longest*.

◆ *The river grew wider.* Use this phrase as a story starter and ask the children to write a story with only a limited number of words, for example 100 or 50.

◆ Ask the children to choose a setting from the picture, for example on the boat, at the campsite, on the train and to write a postcard about what is around them.

◆ Ask the children to imagine they are one of the children cycling along the path on the left of the picture. Tell them to write a letter to a friend or a relative about their journey, telling them where they were going and what they saw along the way.

◆ Tell the children to write a description of the place for someone who has not been to anywhere like it. What descriptive words and phrases will they use? Advise them to write a few sentences, or a short paragraph if they can.

Genre
*labelled
pictorial map*

Gosling
Farm

Tawny Owl Wood

Stumpy's Mill

Mill Lane

Wrigglesworth

Beech Farm

Walter's
Garage

Heronwood Lake

River Dean

Top Acre

Stan's
House

Duncan's
Barn

Pigs'
Field

Milking
Parlour

Cow's
Yard

Bottom Lane

Five Oaks' Field

Spud Field

Middle Field

Owl Wood
Meadow

Riverside
Field

Aunt Ellie's
Willow

Marshy
Wood

Uphill Field

Downhill Field

Whistling
Bridge

River
Rib

Silver
Falls

Goat Common

Colin Reeder (illustration) and Elizabeth Laird (text)

■SCHOLASTIC

Gosling Farm

Geography learning objectives

◆ To use maps and plans (2c).

◆ To identify and describe what places are like (3a).

◆ To make observations about where things are located (4a).

◆ To recognise how places compare with other places (3d).

Background notes

This map is from the endpapers of *The Day Veronica was Nosy* by Colin Reeder and Elizabeth Laird, a story about the youngest calf on Gosling Farm. Gosling Farm occupies the left and centre of this pictorial map. The farmhouse is centre left – Stan's House.

Vocabulary

Acre, yard, parlour, lake, garage, farm, bridge, mountains, barn, lane, hedge.

Discussing the text

◆ Show the picture to the children. What does it show? Is it countryside or a townscape? How do they know? Where was the artist looking from when the picture was painted? The view is of a valley (good flat land for farming) and the hills can be seen on the far side of the valley.

◆ Ask the children if any of them have ever visited somewhere like this. Go through the labels together, showing the children how to sound out any multisyllabic words such as *Her-on-wood*.

◆ Talk about the village called Wrigglesworth. Demonstrate how the letters *Wr* combine to make a different sound from *w* as in *wiggle*. Can the children think of any other words that start with either of these sounds?

◆ Talk about any less familiar words with the children, for example *Parlour*. Have any of the children come across it before? What does it mean? What countryside terms can the children pick out? (For example, *Field*, *River*, *Wood*, *Lake*.)

◆ Talk to the children about the words on the map that have apostrophes in them, for example *Cow's* and *Walter's*. Ask the children if they have seen punctuation marks like this before. Do they know what they are called and why they are used?

◆ Talk to the children about the use of capital letters for the labels. Have the children seen other labels and names like those on the map, for example road names around their home or school?

Geography activities

◆ Examine the map in more detail. List the features the children can see (field, hedges, farm, tractor, village and so on) on a board or flip chart. Use these to develop an awareness of appropriate geographical vocabulary. Ask the children to write a glossary, putting the words into alphabetical order and illustrating each one with a thumbnail sketch. Some children will be able to list them under natural and human features. Remind the children that fields can be considered both natural and human in their creation. What makes a purely natural feature?

◆ Look at the landscape. Draw attention to the hills in the background and the broad valley where the farm is located. Why is the land suitable for farming? (This is flat land, easy to plough and probably quite deep. It is likely to be of good quality, with fine soil washed into and down the valley by the action of rivers in flood. Note that the name *Marshy Wood* suggests that there is still water quite close below the surface in places.) What sort of farming can the children see going on? Give the children access to other farm pictures to look at different farming types in more detail. How might the hills in this landscape be farmed? Why is it more difficult to use machinery on the hills?

◆ Discuss the names in the picture. How might *Middle Field* and *Spud Field*, for example, have got their names? Give groups of children lists of other fields and named features from the map and ask them to work out in their groups why the features have these names. Go on to look at the children's local area in this way. Are there any interesting names for places? Suggest that these can be urban or rural examples.

◆ Talk to the children about directions. Ask them to imagine they are in Gosling Farm, at Stan's House, and have to give directions to Beech Farm. For some children it will be appropriate to remind them of directional vocabulary like *left*, *right* and *straight on* first. Create other routes, such walking from Downhill Field to Heronwood Lake for the children to give directions for these.

◆ Ask the children to identify and count up the different types of transport in the picture. Why would cycling be easy here? Why would it be important to have a car if you lived on the farm? Ask the children to compare the transport here with transport in their own area. Get them to note down what is different and what is similar, and why. What would they have to travel into the town for if they lived at the farm? What could be delivered to the farm?

◆ Help the children to make a wall collage for display. Ask them to choose a section of the picture as the basis for a collage. Which section do they think is a good representative part of the whole picture? (Beech Farm and Walter's Garage to Wrigglesworth with some of the hills beyond might be thought typical – but the children may have better suggestions.)

Further literacy ideas

◆ Use labels as a starting point for looking at proper nouns. Investigate where proper nouns are used. For example for names, addresses, places, signs. Give the children a selection of common nouns and proper nouns and ask them to put capital letters in the appropriate places.

◆ Make a syllables chart of words from the text. Help the children to break the words down and list them under their number of syllables. For example, two-syllable words include *garage* and *river* and three-syllable words are *Heronwood*, *Wrigglesworth* and *Riverside*.

◆ Ask the children to make a list of characters that they can tell live or have lived in this place, for example *Stan*, *Walter*, and *Aunt Ellie*. Then let them choose one of the characters to write a character sketch for. Remind them to use information from the text, such as where the person lives to help them write about what sort of person they are. Less able children could draw and label a picture of the character.

◆ Ask the children to imagine that they are travelling along either in the car or the train and to write about what they see from the window.

◆ Tell the children to imagine they are going to explain what a farm is to someone who has never seen one before. They could perhaps write this as part of a letter to a friend or relative who lives in a town.

◆ The text contains some compound words, for example *Downhill* and *Riverside*. Ask the children to find more examples of these types of words in their reading books, and to separate them into their smaller component words.

◆ Make a day-on-a-farm diary. Ask the children to write either a list of things that they think someone living on a farm might do in one day, for example *milk the cows, feed the pigs*, or a fuller diary entry.

Town and country

Genre
*information
text with
diagrams*

Town

The buses start at the **bus station**.

We find **corner shops** where lots of people live.

We can buy all our food at a **supermarket**.

Many people live in **flats** in the town.

We need large **car parks** near the shops.

We go to the **travel agent** to arrange a holiday.

People can walk, rest and play in the **park**.

Country

The village **pound** was used to keep stray cattle.

Many villages have a **village green**.

Some villages have a **village shop**.

We find **farms** in the countryside.

Sometimes, there is a **duck pond** on the village green.

Most **village schools** are quite small.

It is fun to walk and play in the **woods**.

Town and country

Geography learning objectives

◆ To use geographical vocabulary (2a).

◆ To use maps and symbols (2c).

◆ To recognise how places have become the way they are (3c).

◆ To recognise how places compare with other places (3d).

◆ To identify differences between physical and human features (4b).

◆ To recognise features in contrasting environments (6b).

Background notes

This piece mirrors the style of information books with which children will be familiar, showing the sorts of things we find in the town and in the country.

Vocabulary

Station, corner shop, supermarket, flats, car park, travel agent, village, farm, duck pond, woodland.

Discussing the text

◆ Show each of the pictures in turn and reveal each line of text a few words at a time, asking the children to predict remaining words or phrases, using the picture and the context of the text. For example, *The buses start at the ____, We find ____ in the countryside.* From the suggestions, list words or phrases that would fit just as well into the statements, for example *Many villages have a <u>church</u>.*

◆ Read the text through. Then ask the children to experiment with swapping some of the initial words in the sentences. For example, <u>Many</u> *people live in flats in the town* could become <u>Some</u> *people live in flats in the town.* Are there any occasions where the meaning of the sentence would be altered by changing the first word to, for example *many, all, some, none, every, sometimes, always, never, rarely?*

◆ Ask the children why they think some of the words are in bold. Revise the idea of key words – the most important ones in this context. Show the children another information passage that does not have this kind of highlight and ask the children to suggest what the key words are in that text.

◆ Talk about this text in terms of non-fiction. Do they recognise the genre? What is the text doing? (Informing, telling us about the town and the country and comparing the two.)

◆ Focus on some or all of the places mentioned. Have the children heard of these features before? Have they seen any of them? Can they think of any other features to add to either the town or country list? Encourage the children to think of more than just a variety of shops, for example a library, cinema, train station, office buildings, leisure centre; village hall and so on.

Geography activities

◆ Discuss the different features found in the town and in the country. Explain the term *village pound.* Many villages had these for stray cattle, mostly in use after fields were enclosed by hedges in the 18th and 19th centuries. Then ask the children to sort all of the features into two new groups – natural/physical and human.

◆ Copy the key words and pictures onto card and cut them up. Using these, the children can match pictures and names. If two or more sets are made, encourage the children to play 'Snap'-type games.

◆ Compare the features included in the text with those in the local area. Look at a map and ask the children to find features that are also identified on the chart, as well as others that are specific to your local area only. If your local area is a town, it might be useful to work with the children on a map showing the countryside, so that the children can see the shape and features of a village. If the local area is a village, you may want to ensure the children recognise features of a town. Talk about whether they consider their local area to be a town or a village. Why? Are there features that could be included in both, such as churches?

◆ Take photographs of significant components of your local area and ask the children to: locate them correctly on an enlarged street map; identify those that they pass on the way to and from school; match photographs to written names and words, for example *St Stephen's Church*. Ask the children to make individual lists, in order, of the features that they pass on their way to school and then discuss whether the list of features tells us whether the area is town or countryside – or a bit of both. (Some schools on the edge of town may be lucky enough to have both.)

◆ Ask groups of children to choose whether they would like to create a town or countryside landscape. Use a large floor map or sheet of paper and ask the groups to plot or add a range of features, using Lego or other materials. Stress that they will need to discuss where to locate them and come to group decisions first. Alternatively, a similar exercise could be done individually, with the children imagining and drawing a picture map of either a town or country scene, plotting in as many characteristic features as they can.

Further literacy ideas

◆ Ask the children to complete a comprehension passage based on one of the two lists, including, for example, *Where in a town would you go to arrange a holiday?* Add some questions for more able children that will require them to think beyond the immediate information given in the text. For example *Why do we need large car parks by the shops?*

◆ Using non-fiction books for information, ask the children to write some similarly styled statements about other places, for example a city or a farm. The children could choose one particular picture on which to base their statements. Advise them to include a simple picture with a short sentence explaining what the feature is and what it is used for.

◆ Ask the children to use some or all of the statements from each list to help them write an informative paragraph describing the town or the country. For example, *You will often find a bus station and a train station in a town. A town usually has many different sorts of houses; some of these will be flats.* This could be done in a shared writing session.

◆ Help the children to write a short story based in either a village or a town. Ask them to fill out a story planner for this, making notes about the main plot. On the planner, give the children a list of questions to help them. For example, *Who will be in your story? Why are these characters in this place? What happens to the characters when they are in this place?* Remind them to consider how the typical features of their chosen place may affect the story.

◆ Use the text as a basis for revising parts of speech. Ask the children to look for verbs, for example *start, buy, play,* and to use each verb they find in a correctly structured and punctuated sentence. The same exercise could be done for nouns and adjectives.

◆ Give the children one of the statements and ask them to extend it into a passage, adding more information. For example, *We go to the travel agent to arrange a holiday. Inside a travel agent's you will find lots of brochures with pictures of different places to go on holiday.*

◆ Talk about each of the key words and ask the children to create a glossary or geographical dictionary. This can be done in small groups, each working with a few words, or individually.

CHAPTER 4

Environmental geography

Environmental issues often crop up where human and physical geography meet. At this age, children become aware of their surroundings and begin to take notice of the quality of their environment. They recognise that there are things that help to make our environment pleasant and other things that will make it unpleasant. They also become aware of the fact that we can all affect our environment, for good or bad. An important issue to recognise is who is responsible for managing an environment – usually, there is someone or some organisation with acknowledged responsibility – but, in another way, any person in an environment has a responsibility for it. Appreciation of all of these concepts will start to develop during Key Stage 1.

The children begin to understand what it means to 'look after' places and things, and that if we do not look after something it will begin to change. Usually neglect will cause it to deteriorate, but not all change is for the worse. In a natural setting, changes often lead to improvements and it is quite possible that change will be just that – different, neither intrinsically better nor worse. Of course, 'better' and 'worse' are subjective, and it is important that children begin to recognise that people will have different opinions about environments and issues.

This chapter highlights a number of environmental issues as well as looking at what contributes to the quality of the environment in general. There are really three themes that connect many of the texts – pollution; responsibility; and recycling. The final piece, 'We're Going on a Bear Hunt', looks at a range of environments.

Children who made a difference

Genre
picture story
in a familiar
setting

The children were learning about recycling.

On the way home they saw some discarded bottles.

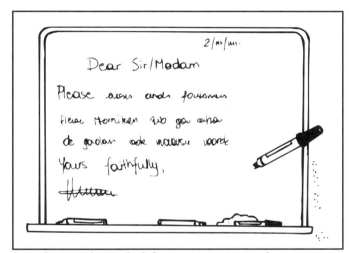

In class, the children wrote a letter to the council.

Dear children. We think your idea is a good one and we propose to put recycling bins in...

The council agreed to provide recycling bins.

Many people started to use them.

They were in the local paper!

Children who made a difference

Geography learning objectives
◆ To understand that individuals can have an effect on an environment (3c, 5a).
◆ To recognise that local councils provide services (5b).

Background notes
This story highlights the opportunities and links with local environmental services that may be available in the area of the school. Understanding about the local council provision of such services is an element of citizenship. Note: you can cut up the copies of this text so that the children can sort it into the correct order.

Vocabulary
Recycling, letter, bottle bank, litter, council, bin, newspaper, local.

Discussing the text
◆ Show the children the pictures without the wording and discuss what the story might be about. Do the children think the text will be part of a fictional story or will it be non-fiction? Use this as an opportunity to discuss the difference between the two, encouraging the children to give examples and characteristics of each type.
◆ Put the cut-up pieces together (but not in order) and discuss the layout of the story – in boxes. Are the elements of the story in the right order? How can we work out the right order? What do the children think happened first?
◆ Once the text is in order, talk about what happens in the story. What have the children in the text been learning about? What do the children in the class know about this topic?
◆ Go back to focusing on the layout of the piece. Do the children think it matters in what order the different sentences are read? Why is this? What can the children suggest to make it clear to the reader that the sentences need to be read in a particular order? (For example, numbering or lettering the boxes.)
◆ Discuss the letter that the children wrote to the council. What would have been included in this letter? Establish whom the letter would be addressed to and where it would have been sent. How might the children have felt when they got the reply? Do the children think it is a good idea to write to the council with their suggestion? Have any of the children ever written a letter like this? Who did they write to and what was it about?
◆ Point out the picture of the newspaper article and talk about the headline. Can the children tell you the purpose of headlines? Help them to appreciate that they are normally set large and bold to catch people's attention.
◆ Talk about the straightforward style of the text. Help the children see that the sentences are quite simple and short as they are only captions for the pictures. Ask the children that if they were writing a story, how would they change the sentences? For example, they might add some interesting descriptive words and vary the length of the sentences.

Geography activities

◆ Emphasise the word *recycling* in the text. What do we mean by *recycling*? What sorts of thing can be recycled? Why is it important to recycle as much as possible?

◆ Talk about your local area. Where are the nearest recycling points to the school and the children's homes? Not all recycling points have bins for everything. Ask the children to list where they would go to recycle specific things – bottles, newspapers, glossy paper, cardboard, telephone directories, clothes, shoes and so on. Do they know of anywhere for recycling old spectacles or mobile phones? Where can you take large items? Is there a collection service for common recyclable materials?

◆ Discuss what the council is and what the members do. What are they responsible for? Ask the children: *If you want to get something done, such as traffic calming or a road resurfaced, or the local park isn't being looked after, who would you contact?* (There are two direct possibilities: the relevant council department or the local councillor; an indirect approach might be through the local paper.)

◆ Discuss the 'other side' of the recycling issue. What happens to our rubbish – the waste that is not recycled? Talk about landfill sites and the difficulty of finding more, the inconvenience to people of a procession of refuse lorries going past. This is also a concern to people living near an incinerator, with the added problems of possible pollution, unpleasant fumes and so on. Is it really a valid choice to dump rubbish at sea? Stress that the more rubbish we make, the more has to be disposed of somehow. Find out how many bags of rubbish are put out each week at home or at school. Is there anything that could be reused or recycled? The children could find out for homework how much rubbish their household puts out, but remind them not to go searching through the rubbish themselves!

◆ Litter is a related problem that might also be looked at. Are there sufficient litter bins provided in the local area? Are they in the best places? Are they used? Devise a trip round the local area as a class, looking at litter and recording on a map where the litter occurs and where the litter bins are, and how well they are used. Make a wall display of the results and talk about whether the litter bins are in the right places. (If they were full, they were in the right place.) Are there any places where another bin would be useful? Think about what might affect the results. (For example, the litter bins may have been emptied just before your visit!)

◆ Brainstorm ways to reuse old CDs and CD-ROMs. Then collect recyclable materials, including these, and help the children to make a collage or posters to put up at school to encourage recycling.

Further literacy ideas

◆ Explore the layout styles of newspapers. Ask the children to come up with alliterative headlines for the news story in the text. These could be written out in different ways on individual whiteboards or on a computer. A further activity would involve giving the children some simple headlines from a newspaper and asking them to predict what these newspaper stories are about.

◆ Use the story to introduce or revise letter-writing conventions. Demonstrate how to set out a letter and give the children a chance to practise this. The activity could be done in shared writing, with all of the children contributing to a class letter. You could possibly write to the headteacher about a school environmental issue that the children have noticed needs tackling.

◆ Talk about narrators and person in story writing, and ask the children to rewrite the story in the first person, as though they had been involved in the action. Encourage them to add more details, for example, *I learned about recycling at school last week.*

◆ Give the children one of the sentences and ask them to expand it so that it makes complete sense on its own, without the context of the other sentences and pictures to help understanding. For example, *Many people started to use the bins that the council put in the park.* Ask the children to underline all those words that they added to their sentences.

Our house, our street

Genre
picture with labels and question/ instruction captions

Our house, our street

Geography learning objectives
◆ To develop observation skills (1b).
◆ To develop understanding of likes and dislikes (1c).
◆ To identify factors that contribute to the urban environment (3c).

Vocabulary
Aerial, chimney, tree, paving, house, satellite dish, street, road, modernise, row.

Discussing the text
◆ Read through each of the text bubbles with the children, discussing the questions. Ask the children to identify those words that tell the reader to do something, for example *Count*. Can the children suggest other words that might be used when giving instructions, for example <u>Tie</u> your shoelaces, <u>Make</u> a bow?

◆ Talk about the question words *how* and *what*. Brainstorm a list of other question words with the children, such as *why, when, where, who* and *which*. Put a list of them on the wall for children to refer to. Practise making questions using these words. Discuss other sentence clues noticeable from reading the text, such as the question mark at the end of a sentence or the way we often raise the pitch at the end of a spoken question. This last one does not always happen, though, and there is a growing tendency for young people to raise the pitch interrogatively at the end of statements, making them sound like questions!

◆ Re-read the whole text together, to check for the children's knowledge of pronunciation and meanings of vocabulary such as *tarmac* and *satellite*. In a guided reading session, the children could answer the questions posed in the text.

◆ The title of the text is 'Our house, our street'. Discuss how the street is similar to or different from the places that the children live in.

◆ Focus on the picture and talk about the way that the houses have been changed. Introduce the term *modernise*. Discuss why people might choose to change their houses and how they might go about doing it.

◆ Address the layout of the text and talk about the text in terms of fiction and non-fiction. Get the children to identify whether this is a fiction or non-fiction piece. Does it tell a story? Does it give information? Does it give instructions?

Geography activities
◆ Examine the row of houses in the picture. Explain that when they were first built, they all looked the same. Are they the same now? What has happened to make them different? Give the children copies of the page and ask them to mark the differences between the houses.

◆ Discuss why people individualise their houses. (Note that this is not necessarily home improvement or repair, but changing their home to make it particularly 'theirs'.) What methods do people use to make their home different? (Examples might be the colour of the panting, cladding, different designs of garden.) Exactly why they do it is another matter, but the straight answer is that they want to make it their own 'special place' in some way.

◆ Tell the children the saying *A house is not a home.* What do we mean by this? Why is it not? Talk about how people make a house into a home. Ask the children to discuss and describe this in groups.

◆ Get the children to debate the sorts of things they like in a street scene, and what they do not like so much. Try to get beyond just the amount of litter and discuss things like people leaving their wheelie bins out, gardens, trees, the amount of parked cars, whether or not there is a lot of traffic, street lighting. Does everybody agree? This could also lead to discussion of trends, including hanging baskets, for instance, or things that might be being sold at the local garden centre or DIY store.

◆ Who likes garden gnomes? Are there some in the gardens along the children's streets? Some people like them, others hate them. The important thing for children to realise – and accept – is that people *do* have different tastes and that this is not necessarily a question of right and wrong.

◆ Notwithstanding the previous discussions, there is likely to be consensus about such things as litter; but talk as well about important items in the street environment, such as street lights, postboxes and bus stops. The last two also indicate services that are provided in the local area. Get the children to talk about other services provided to houses. Is there any evidence of these in the picture? Ask them to list all the indications of services they can see and also others that may be provided. (Obvious evidence includes the television aerials and satellite dishes; less visible services could be cable television and telephone, water and sewage services, gas and electricity.)

◆ For homework, get the children to answer the questions, using the view from one of the windows in their home. These could then be written as reports and compared with other children's responses back in the classroom. You will need to agree in general terms on the viewpoint from which the answers will be given, but take into account the different types of house, flat and so on that the children live in (and whether their downstairs view might be blocked by a high hedge, for example). This activity can lead to a lot of discussion about views, urban or rural landscapes, and specific examples of the street scene elements examined.

Further literacy ideas

◆ Remind the children that all the sentences in the text are questions or instructions. Give the children a list of instruction words (imperative verbs), for example *make*, *undo*, *watch* and *wait*, and ask them to make up a list of instructions using each of the words. Then give the children a list of question words, for example *how*, *why*, *when*, and ask the children to make up questions that include them. Keep within the street scene theme at first, although you may like to develop this to the classroom or school as another familiar context.

◆ Give the children a number of unpunctuated statements and questions and ask them to put in the correct punctuation – full stops, capital letters and question marks.

◆ Use the pictures and the title, 'Our house, our street', in a shared writing lesson to show the children how it is necessary to include detail in order to build up a story setting.

◆ Ask the children to answer the questions posed in the text in full sentences, ensuring that they use correct grammar and punctuation.

◆ Give the children certain letter patterns, such as *ee* and *ow* and ask them to find in the text as many words as they can that contain that pattern. Encourage them to add to these lists words from other texts or reading books.

◆ Write out some of the sentences from the text, but with the words mixed up. Ask the children to rewrite them so that they make sense, for example *trees can you how many see.* More able children could do the mixing up for partners to correct.

◆ Compile a class glossary for the features in the picture. For example, *postbox – where you post your letters, street lamp – a light that helps you see outside your house when it is dark.*

Recycling questionnaire

Reduce — Reuse — Recycle

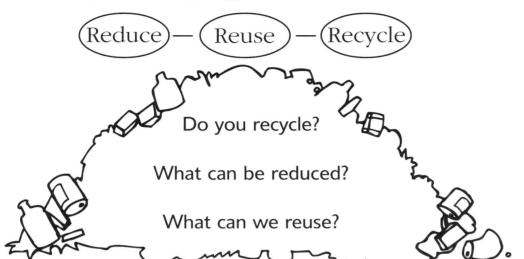

Do you recycle?

What can be reduced?

What can we reuse?

How often do you recycle these household items? (Please tick) ✔

	Daily	Weekly	Monthly	Sometimes	Never
Milk bottles					
Other glass bottles					
Aluminium foil					
Aluminium cans					
Newspapers/ magazines/ other paper					
Clothes					

Recycling questionnaire

Geography learning objectives

◆ To recognise the importance of waste processing (3c).

◆ To understand that we can all contribute to the reduction of waste (5b).

◆ To recognise that reduction and reuse are at least as important as recycling (5a, 5b).

Background notes

This is a very different type of text, as it is designed to gather information. It is a simple example that the children can use easily. They could also use it as a model when designing their own questionnaires. As well as being a major geographical theme, the questionnaire identifies an element of citizenship through personal understanding of, and responsibility for, reduction, reuse and recycling of waste.

Vocabulary

Reduce, reuse, recycle, waste, dump, litter, rubbish, sustainable, toxic, landfill.

Discussing the text

◆ What type of text is this? Ask the children what we call this sort of sheet and establish their understanding of the term *questionnaire*. What is the purpose of a questionnaire? Who would use something like this? What could they do with the information collected? Ask the children if they have ever been asked to fill in a questionnaire like this. What was it about?

◆ Talk about the layout of the text – why it is set out like this. What would be the effect of, for example, not having the boxes? Talk about the need to keep different bits of information separate. Can the children suggest another way that the information could be laid out? They could draw their suggestions on individual or group whiteboards.

◆ At the top of the page, there is a slogan *Reduce–Reuse–Recycle*. Talk about the purpose and construction of slogans. Why are they used and where? Talk about the effect they have on the reader. Does this slogan catch the eye and make the reader want to read more?

◆ Read through the text and ensure that the children are familiar with all of the vocabulary, for example *household*, *reduced*.

◆ Draw the children's attention to the punctuation used – the question marks in particular.

◆ Ask the children to consider the text overall and suggest any improvements that they think could or should be made to it. For example, is the instruction *Please tick* clear enough or does it need to be a full sentence? Emphasise the need to keep things simple and avoid being 'wordy', and the possibility of shortage of space. Would people fill in a questionnaire if it were over a page long?

◆ Discuss the meanings of the different timescales given in the questionnaire. Do the children understand what each means? Can they see that the boxes go from most frequent to least frequent; that *Sometimes* here means less than once a month? Can they suggest other words we use for relatively short, regular periods of time (for example, *fortnightly*, *annually*), or for irregular periods (perhaps *occasionally*)?

Geography activities

◆ Talk about the three main words – *reduce, reuse* and *recycle*. Have they come across them together before? What is the difference between them? Go through the distinctions. Reduce – what can be reduced? Discuss unnecessary packaging, for example. Reducing this reduces the final waste and the amount manufactured in the first place, thus saving the initial energy costs of production. Reuse – if it cannot be reduced, since it has been made, make as much use of it as possible before discarding it. Recycle – as the last stage, this makes the best use of a truly 'used' product, so that it can 'reappear', either in the same basic form or as something very different. *Recycling* covers everything from our kitchen waste ending up as good compost to aluminium saucepans ending up as aeroplane components – perhaps even the metal from an old car ending up in a children's toy car.

◆ We talk about *recycling*, but if the children think about how milk bottles or clothes, for instance, are 'recycled' then they will realise that it is often *reuse*. Get them to find out which items on the chart are recycled and what they might become.

◆ Discuss some of the environmental effects of too much waste being generated – the need for landfill sites, incinerators, dumping at sea and unsightly fly-tipping, but also the additional use of natural resources. For example, generating new paper instead of recycling it means more trees and more energy are used in manufacturing.

◆ Ask the children to find out what we mean by *sustainable sources*. For example, woodland being replaced one-for-one as trees are cut down and a sufficient area being planted to sustain use over a long period. The children should discover that if we then continue cutting down trees, but keep the area the same, eventually there will be no more mature trees in the plantation.

◆ Help the children to identify where their nearest recycling point is for each of the items on the questionnaire. Remind them that charity shops can be seen as recycling points, although giving away items in this way is really a form of reuse.

◆ Ask the children to fill in the questionnaire for homework and then talk about the results as a class. With the children's help, draw a graph of the results and discuss what it shows. Talk about how people might respond to questionnaires like this one. Would they, for instance, tend to overestimate or underestimate how much they recycle? Talk about *why*, for example that people's memories are not always accurate on this sort of occasion and, although people may not consciously falsify, there may be a tendency to err on the side of 'feeling good' about how much they recycle.

Further literacy ideas

◆ Give the children a selection of newspapers and magazines and ask them to record any slogans they come across. Tell them to record what the slogan was used to advertise or encourage. Ask the children to invent their own slogans for particular products or initiatives, for example to encourage healthy eating.

◆ *Reduce–Reuse–Recycle*. Use this slogan to start work on alliteration. Challenge the children to write phrases that include a specified number of words that alliterate, for example *the slimy, slippery slow worm*. Encourage the children to put some of these alliterative lines into poems.

◆ Give the children a topic, for example exercise habits, and ask them to think of questions that someone could be asked on it, such as *How often do you exercise?* Remind the children to use question marks. As a shared or guided writing lesson, transfer this information into a questionnaire.

◆ Investigate the suffix *-ly*. Ask the children to write down the root words in *weekly* and *monthly* and then find other words to which they can add *-ly* (for example, *surely, fairly* and so on). Point out any words like *daily*, where the root word – *day* – needs to be altered before adding *-ly*. If the children are ready for it, you may want to explain that these are all adverbs.

Carbreakers

Genre
*descriptive
poem with
rhythm and
an ABCB
rhyming
pattern*

There's a graveyard in our street,
But it's not for putting people in;
The bodies that they bury here
Are made of steel and tin.

The people come and leave their wrecks
For crunching in the giant jaws
Of a great hungry car-machine,
That lives on bonnets, wheels and doors.

When I pass by the yard at night,
I sometimes think I hear a sound
Of ghostly horns that moan and whine,
Upon that metal-graveyard mound.

Marian Lines

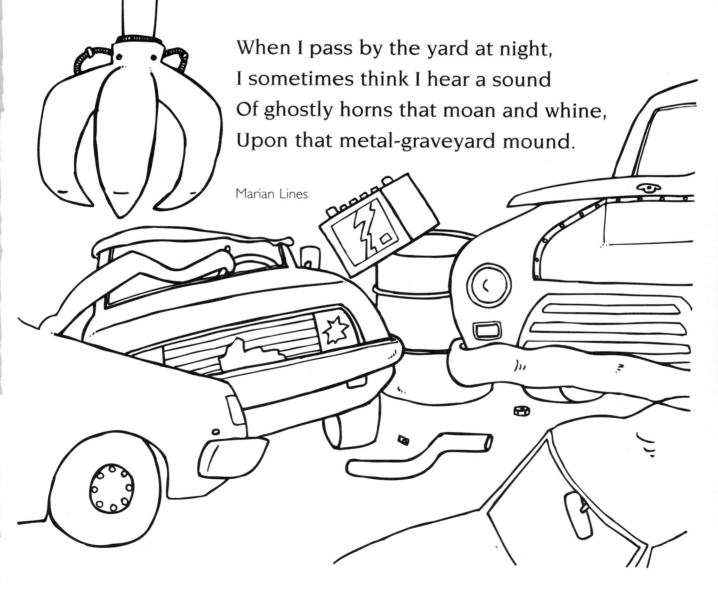

Carbreakers

Geography learning objectives

◆ To express views about places and the environment (1c).

◆ To describe what a place is like (3a).

◆ To recognise how a place is changing (3c).

◆ To recognise how the environment can be improved (5b).

Background notes

This short poem is on a recycling theme, but it also raises issues of other aspects of the environment. You may like to discuss with the children whether or not they think a scrapyard is a good idea, and then talk about what it is for. Then ask them how they would feel about having a scrapyard in their street. You could go on to talk about cars that are sometimes left at the side of the road as 'rubbish', and how the children feel about these.

Vocabulary

Graveyard, street, bodies, steel, wrecks, crunching, machine, wheels, yard, metal, material.

Discussing the text

◆ Perhaps just show the children the first line and ask them to predict what the poem is about. Advise them to use the title as a clue. Read on through the first verse and discuss with the children why the poet has used the term *graveyard* to describe the breaker's yard. Go into more detail on what the children can tell from this first verse on what the poem is about. Do the children know what a scrapyard is? Has anyone been around one? Do they know what happens in a scrapyard?

◆ Read the poem through with the children a couple of times. Talk about expression and intonation and then re-read the poem together, taking these things into account. You may choose to give a different group of children each verse to read or underline the parts of the poem that you want emphasised in each reading. Explain any unfamiliar words or difficult images, such as *wrecks*, *giant jaws*, *car-machine*.

◆ Choose sentences from the poem to display, covering the last words. Then ask the children to try to remember the words used by the poet, for example *The people come and leave their ___.* *I sometimes think I hear a ___.*

Geography activities

◆ Discuss with the children why the poem talks about a car graveyard. What has happened to the cars? When people want to buy a new car what happens to the old one they have? Explain the chain of buying a car and reselling or scrapping the previous one. The children can also take the opportunity to examine the different materials used in the parts of a car, so they realise that the high content of plastics, glass and metal would make it difficult to dispose of easily.

◆ Explore with the children why so many people like (or need) to use cars as often as they do. What are the advantages and disadvantages? How do the children themselves come to school?

You may have already created a graph to show the ways in which they travel and this can be revisited to explore the results in this context. Is there a 'walking bus' scheme in operation at the school? If not, find out information from your LEA who will know of schools in your area involved in such schemes. Is it possible to organise one at the school for perhaps one day a week if not all the time?

◆ Discuss with the class how traffic affects your local area. Are there particular parts that have congestion or parking problems? Encourage the children to carry out an enquiry piece of work such as the example given in the QCA Schemes of Work unit 'How can we make our local area safer?', which looks at the problems of parking near school.

◆ Talk about the issues of reusing and recycling. What is the difference? Discuss this with specific relation to cars. Explain how a car is *reused* by being sold on to another owner or used for another purpose (see below); and how it is *recycled* by the scrap-dealer extracting the spare parts and as many of the materials as possible, and selling those on to people who can use the metal, for instance, to make other things. Then go on to ask what sorts of other items can be reused. The children's clothes when they have outgrown them? Baby clothes? Milk bottles? Make a list together of the things that are reused or recycled in school (perhaps containers for equipment or materials, yoghurt pots for painting and growing things, calendar pictures on the wall). Give the children a list of objects including stamps, newspapers, plastic and cardboard boxes, Christmas cards, and ask them to suggest ways of reusing or recycling them.

◆ Ask the children to think of imaginative ways of reusing or recycling a car. An example of reuse you might give them is that French farmers sometimes use an old car for their hens to roost in!

◆ Based on the poem, create a large breaker's yard collage for display in the corridor or classroom. Ask the children for suggestions on what recycled and reused materials they could use.

Further literacy ideas

◆ Point out the words *there's* and *it's* in the poem and introduce or revise contractions. Ask the children to think of a list of contractions and what they are short for, for example *don't – do not*.

◆ Use the metaphor *great hungry car-machine* as the title for a poem. Start the work by asking the children to brainstorm a list of additional words to describe this machine.

◆ Ask the children to list all the rhyming words in the poem, for example *jaws – doors*. Then tell them to add at least one other rhyming word to each of the pairs, for example *in – tin – bin*. More able children could then compare where the letter patterns in these rhyming words are the same and where they are different.

◆ Write out the poem in the form of a cloze procedure and ask the children either to choose suitable words from a list given by you or to think of their own.

◆ See if the children can write a poem in a similar style for a dustbin lorry. Ask the children to use the example of crunching jaws from the poem and to give the lorry some human or animal features.

◆ Ask the children to write the poem out in a shape appropriate to the content; once designed, it could be written out in neat for display, as a handwriting activity. Get the children to find other examples of poems about cars and to write these out as well to produce a themed class anthology.

◆ Help the children to learn the poem to recite it as a class. In an early practice, decide together where the children need to add expression and intonation to their performance. You could add percussion instruments and choose a suitable audience for the performance, for example parents or a school assembly.

Rules for the playground

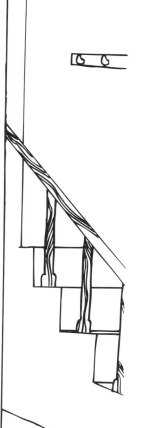

- Always walk into the playground from your classroom.

- Take care when running.

- Don't bump into anyone.

- Help anyone who falls over.

- Only play ball games in the lower playground.

- Always keep away from the car park.

- Find an adult if you need help.

- Listen for the whistle.

- Line up quietly at the end of playtime.

These rules are really to help everyone to

ENJOY PLAYTIME SAFELY!

Rules for the playground

Geography learning objectives

◆ To express views about how people should respond to the environment (1c).

◆ To use fieldwork skills (2b).

◆ To make maps and plans (2e).

◆ To make observations about where things are located and other features in the environment (4a).

◆ To recognise how an environment could be improved (5b).

Background notes

The school grounds provide a rich environment for early work in geography, and rules for the playground provide an introduction to the rationale, for example, of the Country Code used in the wider environment. This all makes a significant contribution to early work on citizenship.

Vocabulary

Playground, bump, car park, playtime, quietly, access.

Discussing the text

◆ At first, show the children just the title – 'Rules for the playground'. What do they think that the text is going to be about? What is its aim? How do they expect the text to be set out? They could record some ideas on individual whiteboards. Show the children the text and ask them about the bullet points. Introduce this term if they are unfamiliar with it. Why do the children think these are used? Have they seen them anywhere else and, if so, where?

◆ Read the rules through with the children and discuss the language used. Try to introduce the idea of more formal language being used for this type of text. Do the children think the text sounds quite 'serious'? Why?

◆ Where might we see this type of text? Have the children seen other rules? Where were they? Were they written in the same way? If they were written differently, how were they different? (Swimming pool rules, for instance, often have pictures to accompany them.) Do the children think these rules would benefit from pictures? Would any of the points be clearer with a diagram? What about very young children – would they be able to understand them? How could the rules be made accessible to everyone who needed to know about them?

◆ Discuss the words in capital letters at the end of the text. Why are they written like this? Talk about the exclamation mark. Introduce the children to this piece of punctuation if they are not already familiar with it. What is its effect? Ask the children to give examples of other places (including fiction) where they might see an exclamation mark.

Geography activities

◆ Stress the importance of following rules in the playground. How do these improve the quality of the environment for everyone? Are there any rules that the children think should be added to or taken away from the list here? How do these rules compare with ones for their own playground? Ask the children to write down what they remember the school's playground rules to be. Do they always follow them?

◆ If the school does not have playground rules as such, take the children out for a walk round and discuss rules that would be worth having. Are there any special aspects that need to be considered? (Balls into neighbours' gardens, separate playgrounds, footpaths, parked cars and so on.)

◆ Ask the children to think about people who might not be able to read these rules, for example younger children who cannot read very well or children for whom English is a second language or whose sight is impaired. How could we give them access to the information? Ask the children to design a poster predominantly using symbols, with only a few simple words to explain them. They could also practise recording readings of the rules on a tape recorder.

◆ Take the children out into the playground and discuss aesthetic improvements that could be made, for example painting a scene on a wall, putting plants or flowers around the playground, marking games or a compass on the ground. Draw attention to the shape of the playground. Back in the classroom, small groups can discuss ideas and perhaps conduct some research for other children's opinions, and produce suitable designs to show in assembly or at a school council meeting.

Further literacy ideas

◆ Give the children a copy of the rules and ask them to underline the specific words that are giving instruction (the imperative verbs), for example *Find, Listen, Help, Don't*. Point out that the verb is not necessarily at the start of the sentence – look at *keep* and *play*. Ask the children to put these words in their spelling logs and learn them using Look–Say–Cover–Write–Check.

◆ As part of a shared writing lesson, devise some similar rules for another situation that is familiar to the children, for example *Rules for dinner time*.

◆ Ask the children to write a short story about someone who decided to break one of the playground rules. Encourage the children to plan their story first and write it over a couple of lessons. It may be helpful to do this activity as a guided writing session using a prepared story planner that requires the children to plan the beginning, middle and end of their story.

◆ Use the word *don't* from the text to introduce or revise simple contractions with the children. Give them a list of contractions, for example *shouldn't, we've, you're* and *I'll*, and ask the children to write down the full version of the phrase; or give them phrases to contract.

◆ Talk to the children about positive and negative language. As a guided reading session, re-read the rules together and ask the children to try to identify which of them contain positive words. For example, <u>Always</u> *keep away from the car park* is positive. Can they suggest how this could be written in a negative way but with the same emphasis? (For example, <u>Never</u> *go near the car park*.) This activity can also be reversed so that negative statements like *Don't bump into anyone* can be changed to be more positive, for example *Make sure that you always look where you're going*.

◆ Ask the children to write a playground guide which expands on the rules. They could make a small booklet that gives reasons for each of the rules. For example, *Take care when running. If you don't you may fall over and hurt yourself. You might also bump into someone else and you could both get hurt.*

◆ Use words from the text to investigate compound words, such as *playtime* and *playground*. Challenge the children to find other words with a component word in common. Make lists of words containing *play, ground, time* and so on. Note that some words will appear in more than one list.

ENVIRONMENTAL GEOGRAPHY

The Country Code

Keep to public rights
of way across farmland.

Use gates and stiles to cross
fences and walls

Guard against all risks of fire.

Help to keep all water clean.

Protect wildlife, plants and trees.

Take your litter home.

Leave livestock, crops and
machinery alone.

Enjoy the countryside and respect
its life and work.

Take special care on
country roads.

Keep your dogs under
close control!

Make no unnecessary noise.

Fasten all gates.

The Country Code

Geography learning objectives

◆ To use geographical vocabulary (2a).

◆ To use secondary sources of information (2d).

◆ To relate the Country Code to a range of places (3c, 5a).

◆ To recognise how places compare with other places (3d).

◆ To recognise how the Country Code helps to protect the environment (5b).

Background notes

The Country Code is a well-established set of rules for all people who go into the countryside. It is designed to help protect the countryside from unnecessary damage while at the same time raising awareness of the countryside. Codes that identify the importance of rules to protect aspects of society, such as the countryside environment, offer an opportunity to develop links to curriculum areas like PSHE and citizenship.

Vocabulary

Code, public, farmland, machinery, stile, hedge, control, wildlife, litter, livestock, countryside, fasten, risk, right of way, protect.

Discussing the text

◆ Read through the text with the children and discuss any unfamiliar terms or vocabulary, for example *public rights of way, unnecessary*.

◆ Look at the heading and discuss the term *Country Code*. Why do the children think this text is called a code? Can they think of any other sort of code? (For example, the Green Cross Code.) What is the purpose of a code? Where would you find one? Who writes something like this and who is it for? Introduce the children to the idea of a public information document. What other sorts of public documents do the children know about?

◆ Examine the punctuation in the text. Most of the lines are straightforward sentences. Why do the children think that one of the points has an exclamation mark by it? Point out the commas used to separate items within a list.

◆ Talk about the style of the language in this document – it is very firm and formal. Why do the children think this is?

◆ Discuss the children's experience of being in the countryside. Have they had to follow any of these rules before? Why do they think it is important to have a code like this for the country? Emphasise the need for *protection* of such places.

◆ Talk about the genre with the children. Establish that it is non-fiction. What is its purpose? (To tell people what to do and how to behave properly when they are in out the country. It gives information in the form of instructions.)

◆ Ask the children to pick out the key words and underline their suggestions on your shared text. Can the children recognise any similarities between some of words underlined? Are they instruction verbs, that tell you to do things, for example *Keep* and *Fasten*?

Geography activities

◆ Discuss reasons for having a code for the countryside. Why do people visit the countryside? Is this code for local people or for visitors? Which points might apply to both?

◆ Ask the children to consider why each point is important. What, for example, would be the outcome of not fastening the gate, or playing on machinery in a field? Working in groups, get each group to take one point from the Code and write down the reason for it. Display these on the wall.

◆ Ask the children to write out the Code, with the lines widely spaced apart, and then provide an illustration for each point. This could be designed, for example, as a poster or bookmark.

◆ Discuss with the children the other sorts of code which are available, such as the Highway Code. What are the best ways of getting people to read and understand them? (Short points, easy to read, sensible points, diagrams and so on.)

◆ As a class, make a corresponding set of rules for the town or city – an urban code – after discussing some of the issues that would arise in towns. Will some of the points be the same for both places? (For example, relating to dogs, trees and litter.) The children may come up with many issues and it will be important to negotiate recognition of the most important ones. Why would a list of 20 points in a code be unhelpful?

◆ Cut up the Code into its points and shuffle their order. Give each group of children a set and ask them to put them in order of *priority*. Which are the most and least important to protect the countryside? Each group should then present their choices and explain why they came to these decisions.

Further literacy ideas

◆ Look at the sentence construction of the points and the key words the children suggested earlier. Give the children a copy of the Code and ask them to cross out those words in each instruction that they think are not so important. For example, *Fasten all gates* could become *Fasten gates*. Are there any occasions where taking out one of the words changes the meaning? For example, is *Make no noise* the same as *Make no unnecessary noise*?

◆ Give the children the instructions with the words muddled up and ask them to sort them so that they make sense. More able children may be able to find examples where it is possible to change some of the order of the sentence and it still makes sense. For example, *Protect wildlife, plants and trees* could be written as *Protect trees, wildlife and plants*.

◆ Use the text as a starting point for work on how commas are included in lists of words. Give the children lots of nouns related to the countryside and/or the city and ask them to use lists of them in sentences, putting commas in the correct places.

◆ Ask the children to pick a couple of the points – perhaps from a bag so that they are unseen, and ask them to create a 100-word story that includes the importance of that instruction in some way. They could write, for instance, a story that involves a fire in the countryside.

◆ Identify some of the verbs in the text, for example *Make, Keep, Help*, and ask the children to complete sentences that begin with these words.

◆ Ask the children to write a descriptive poem set in the countryside. Encourage them to use their senses as much as possible and to use adventurous vocabulary so that the reader can build up a picture in his or her mind.

◆ As part of a shared or guided writing lesson, write a full code on how people should behave in the town or the city. Start by using some of the rules the children thought of for the urban code if you have done that activity. Ask the children to write these codes out with illustrations or use word-processing or desktop publishing tools to experiment with different fonts and layout positions so that the instructions have an impact on the reader.

Bucket and spade

Genre
*information
with elements
of argument*

It's fun to spend a day at the seaside. If we leave anything behind, it becomes pollution on the beach.

Some things belong on the seashore. These are natural things, such as sand, rocks and pebbles. There may also be living plants, animals or their remains washed up by the sea.

Some things do not belong in the sea or on the shore. Tin cans and plastic bottles are rubbish left behind by people. They cause pollution.

Text reproduced by permission of Hodder and Stoughton Limited

TEACHERS'
NOTES

Bucket and spade

Geography learning objectives

◆ To identify natural and intrusive material in an environment (4a, 4b).
◆ To understand why pollution poses problems (5a).

Background notes

The seaside is a familiar environment to most children, and one that is associated with relaxation and fun. This text raises the issue of pollution of beaches and our role in causing it, through leaving things behind when we leave. This is just a starting point…

Vocabulary

Pollution, beach, seaside, natural, remains, rubbish, litter.

Discussing the text

◆ Read the first sentence of the text and then ask the children to talk about times they have spent at the seaside. What did they do there, who did they go with and when did they go? What was the weather like? Ask the children to predict what they think the rest of the text is about. Is it a fiction or non-fiction piece? What tells us this? (The opening sentence is factual and in the present tense implying that this is going to be a non-fiction text of information. Stories rarely have openings similar to this.) Can the children suggest any other texts that they know of (non-fiction and fiction) that are about the seaside?

◆ Read and discuss the second sentence of the text. What sort of things do the children think might be left behind on the beach? Use the picture to get some ideas, but encourage the children to tell you from experience about anything they or their families have left behind by mistake.

◆ Read through the rest of the text together, then ask the children to suggest which are the key words or phrases in the text, for example *leave behind*, *pollution*, *natural*.

◆ Cover up parts of the text and ask the children to suggest what words are hidden, for example *These are natural things, such as sand, rocks and ___.* Can the children suggest different words from those used that might fit in context?

Geography activities

◆ Encourage the children to talk about their memories of visits to the seaside. Who has been? What was the beach like? What did they do on the beach? How were they dressed? Did they have shoes and socks on all the time? Was there any rubbish on the beach? Was the beach a pleasant place to be? Why?

◆ Brainstorm a list of objects and features that might be found on a beach. Use a board or flip chart to list them under the headings *Belongs* and *Does not belong*. The text gives a few examples of each to get the children started.

◆ Look at the *Does not belong* list and ask the children to sort the items into various categories, for example *unsightly*, *dangerous to people*, *harmful to animals*. Suggest that they may want to list some items in more than one category.

◆ What happens to pollution on the beach? Explain that some of it will be washed higher up the beach, up to or beyond the tideline; some will be washed away by the sea. What might happen to the rubbish that is washed away? (Give the children a clue – *Where does some of the rubbish found on the beach come from?*) Does washing away the rubbish solve the problem or just give it to someone else?

◆ Make a collection of rubbish from your school grounds or local area. (NB Take care to use protective gloves and avoid collecting potentially dangerous/toxic products.) Get the children to help you classify the items into *man-made* or *natural*, then reclassify them into *Still here in one-year's time* or *Not existing in one-year's time*. This introduces the idea of biodegradability. Many things rot away as part of the natural cycle of life. Discuss how long it would take plastic or broken glass to pass back into the natural environment – if ever! (This exercise is much better done on a beach if possible, but is of course perfectly possible in school.)

◆ Help the children to make a seaside collage, split into two sections – one with a clean, unpolluted beach and the other with various types of pollution. Ask the children to make labels for the collage.

◆ Can we always see pollution? Discuss with the children what happens if waste is washed into water. It may seem to disappear, but it is often still there. You can illustrate this in class with water and detergent – if it is allowed to dissolve carefully, then it will seem to 'disappear', but a quick stir, or smell of the container, will tell you that it has not gone away. Talk about safe bathing and the Blue Flag scheme, which is a scheme to indicate that a beach has met certain standards of cleanliness for bathing purposes. (By late 2001, most beaches in the UK had met European standards for cleanliness.) You could let the children find out about the scheme, what its standards are and where their nearest Blue Flag beach is.

Further literacy ideas

◆ Ask the children to complete a three-column table about the information in the text, with the titles *What do we know already? What do we want to find out? What have we found out?* Advise the children to use non-fiction books to help them find out more about the seaside and pollution. Encourage them to use the contents and index pages of these reference books.

◆ Complete a flow diagram using the text, showing how pollution occurs, including, for example, *people to the beach – eat picnics – drop litter...* Ask the children to complete similar diagrams for outings to other places that they might make.

◆ Ask the children to look again at the facts they have learned from the text and other reference sources. Ask them to retell a number of facts in their own words for another child. More able children might then make index and contents pages for individual, group or class books.

◆ Tell the children to use information from the text to help in writing a letter about the problems of seaside pollution to a newspaper or an important person.

◆ Ask the children to complete a simple review of one of the texts used in the above activity. How easy was it to find the information they wanted? Did it provide additional interesting information? Less able children could be given a sentence to start their review, for example *This text is about...*

◆ Devise differentiated comprehension questions about the passage, for example *What things belong on the beach?* More able children could devise their own questions.

◆ To reinforce their understanding, ask the children to write a straightforward non-fiction account about pollution on the beach. Advise them to base their reports on the main text, but to use their own words and include any additional information they have found out from other sources.

◆ Encourage the children to use the photograph as the setting for a story.

We're Going on a Bear Hunt

Genre
*story with
predictable
and
patterned
language*

Back through the snowstorm! Hoooo wooooo! Hoooo wooooo!

Back through the forest! Stumble trip! Stumble trip! Stumble trip!

Back through the mud! Squelch squerch! Squelch squerch!

Back through the river! Splash splosh! Splash splosh! Splash splosh!

Back through the grass! Swishy swashy! Swishy swashy!

Michael Rosen (text) and Helen Oxenbury (illustration)

We're Going on a Bear Hunt

Geography learning objectives
◆ To use geographical vocabulary (2a).
◆ To use maps (2c).
◆ To identify and describe what places are like (3a).
◆ To recognise how places change (3c).
◆ To recognise a variety of features (4a).

Background notes
This well-known story is a favourite with children and raises awareness of many environments. It is well suited to being acted out and adapted to other environments while still keeping the structured language.

Vocabulary
Cave, snowstorm, forest, mud, river, grass, tunnel, road, environment.

Discussing the text
◆ Read through the text with the children and discuss how reading with expression and intonation can add to the effectiveness of text to the reader or listener. Experiment with using different intonation for the same piece of text to see how it changes the effect of the poem. Can the children read it in an excited way? In a bored way? In a frightened way? And so on. Split the class into groups and ask them to read different parts of the poem, with each group using a different tone of voice.
◆ Discuss whether this text is a poem or a story, or both. Talk about the different characteristics of poems and stories. Do all poems rhyme? Do stories never have rhythm? Do the children know of any other texts where there are repeated phrases like *Swishy swashy! Swishy swashy!*?
◆ Have the children noticed all the exclamation marks? Do they add to the excitement? Discuss how the poem would sound without the exclamation marks.
◆ Discuss the word *squerch*. Is this a word that the children have heard before? Why do they think the author has decided to use this word? (Emphasise the sounds Michael Rosen is reproducing.) Can the children think of any other poems or stories that include made-up words? (Edward Lear's poems are full of them.)
◆ Discuss where the children think the characters have been. What do they think happened in the story before this part of the text? Direct the children to the bear in each picture. The family must have disturbed him, but is he chasing the family to frighten them or be friends with them?

Geography activities
◆ Discuss the different types of environment shown in the pictures and text. What are the characteristics of each? Make a list of these and other environments on a flip chart and add the children's descriptive words alongside.
◆ Take each of the places in turn and ask the children to think about the difficulties of moving through each one. For example, the forest is dark and there are lots of branches; feet get stuck in the mud; it is hard to walk quickly through water and to keep from falling over.

◆ Ask the children to identify some other environments and ways of travelling in them, for example *…down the mountainside* or *…along the twisting alley* and then act out their travels, miming the movements through any difficulties they have identified. This is best done as a small-group activity, where children can brainstorm the ideas.

◆ Have the children ever been to a place like one of those in the story? Where was it? What was it like? When was it? How will the place change from day to night, from summer to winter? Talk about how time and season influence 'atmosphere'. Children can choose on environment and, in two sections, draw the environment by day and by night. Ask them to write one or two sentences underneath each one to describe the feeling of the place. Alternatively, they could divide the paper into four sections and do the same activity but describing the atmosphere at different seasons.

◆ Can the children identify any of these environments in their own locality? Ask them to name them and describe what they are like. How do they differ from the views in the pictures?

◆ Take the children through ways to rewrite the story to set it in their local area. Ask them to select some different places to include, such as a busy road, a tunnel, a shopping centre or a village green. How can they convey the atmosphere in a short descriptive way?

◆ Look at a map of the local area. Can the children identify different places such as woods, towns, rivers, seaside? Give them start and end points and ask them to imagine they walked from one place to the other. What different sorts of places would they pass through? You could then go on to ask the children to act out the whole story, using all the ideas which they have generated about the difficulties involved in various environments.

Further literacy ideas

◆ As a sequencing exercise, present the children with the extract separated into different sections. Mix the sections up and ask the children to put them in the right order. You will need to make sure that the children are familiar with the rest of the story before doing this.

◆ If you have copies of the book, practise reading the whole poem. Add movements and mime as well, as this story lends itself well to this. Add percussion instruments to emphasise the rhythm of the poem and try acting it out as part of a dance lesson. Make use of words and sounds that have been suggested by the children in other activities to add realism to the mime.

◆ Ask the children to think of some different sound words for the environments gone through in the extract. For example, for mud – *slip slop*.

◆ Help the children to change some of the settings but keep the rhythm and style of the sentences in the story, for example *Back through the jungle*.

◆ By contrast, see if the children can change some of the lines, for example *Back through the forest… Back through the mud!*, into longer sentences without any rhythm or pattern – *When we had made it through the forest we had to squelch through the mud.*

◆ Ask the children to create their own poem about a journey, based on this model. For example, *Back along the road…, Back round the corner…*

◆ The poem uses the word *Back* repeatedly. Ask the children to suggest alternative words that could be used on occasions in the poem, such as *On* or *Up*. Read the poem aloud together, using some of these alternatives.

◆ Let the children make a collection of other poems or stories with repeated, patterned text.

◆ Encourage the children to create a sound poem using words in the extract, such as *swishy swashy*.

Geographical skills

The development of geographical skills goes hand in hand with the development of knowledge and understanding. The three are interlinked and each is equally important. The skills which children develop during the primary stage are those of enquiry, of obtaining information from a variety of sources, both primary (firsthand) sources and secondary, and the skills of interpretation and presentation of information acquired.

Many of the geographical skills are practical ones, which need to be practised in the school grounds, in the local area and on visits farther afield. However, there are certain skills that can be developed in the classroom and are literacy in their nature. These are mainly skills of obtaining information from various materials, and knowing how to use contents and index pages. The following texts can serve as an introduction to the skills, or as a way of revising and practising them. They should then be applied in the children's geographical work to reinforce the development of the skill in context. Working this way will also reinforce the literacy aspect as well, in a different context.

The texts in this chapter give examples for ways of obtaining information from text and a pictorial map ('Longleat'), from a street guide ('Cops and Robbers'), from a story to produce a map ('Going to the country'), information from a dictionary and practice of the use of the contents and index pages from an atlas.

Genre
pictorial map
with labels
and captions
– persuasive
presentation

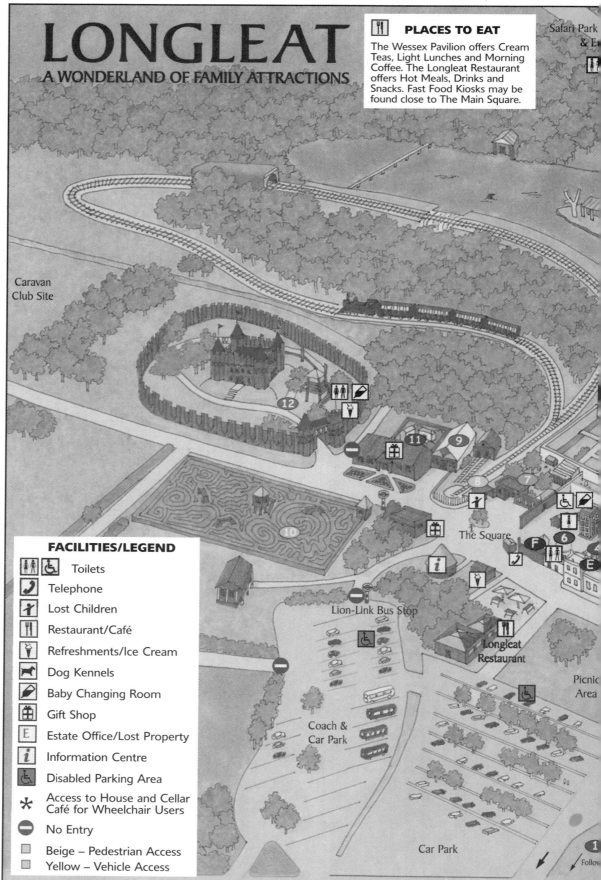

LONGLEAT
A WONDERLAND OF FAMILY ATTRACTIONS

PLACES TO EAT
The Wessex Pavilion offers Cream Teas, Light Lunches and Morning Coffee. The Longleat Restaurant offers Hot Meals, Drinks and Snacks. Fast Food Kiosks may be found close to The Main Square.

Safari Park & E

Caravan Club Site

FACILITIES/LEGEND

Toilets	
Telephone	
Lost Children	
Restaurant/Café	
Refreshments/Ice Cream	
Dog Kennels	
Baby Changing Room	
Gift Shop	
E	Estate Office/Lost Property
i	Information Centre
Disabled Parking Area	
*	Access to House and Cellar Café for Wheelchair Users
	No Entry
	Beige – Pedestrian Access
	Yellow – Vehicle Access

The Square

Lion-Link Bus Stop

Longleat Restaurant

Coach & Car Park

Picnic Area

Car Park

Follow

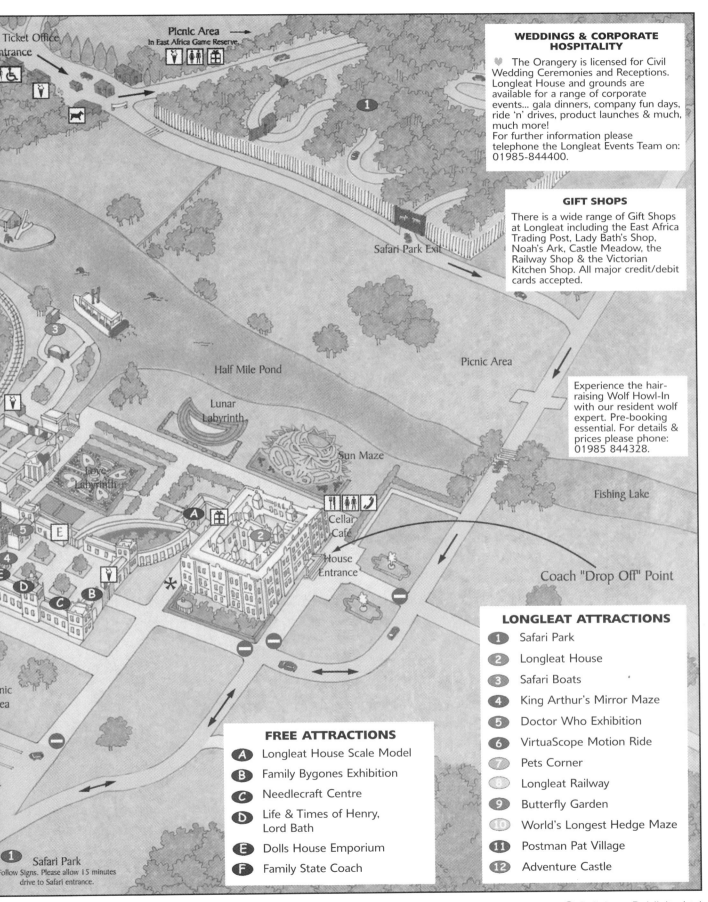

Ticket Office Entrance

Picnic Area →
In East Africa Game Reserve.

Safari Park Exit

Half Mile Pond

Lunar Labyrinth

Sun Maze

Love Labyrinth

Cellar Café

House Entrance

Picnic Area

Fishing Lake

Coach "Drop Off" Point

1 Safari Park
Follow Signs. Please allow 15 minutes drive to Safari entrance.

WEDDINGS & CORPORATE HOSPITALITY

The Orangery is licensed for Civil Wedding Ceremonies and Receptions. Longleat House and grounds are available for a range of corporate events... gala dinners, company fun days, ride 'n' drives, product launches & much, much more!
For further information please telephone the Longleat Events Team on: 01985-844400.

GIFT SHOPS

There is a wide range of Gift Shops at Longleat including the East Africa Trading Post, Lady Bath's Shop, Noah's Ark, Castle Meadow, the Railway Shop & the Victorian Kitchen Shop. All major credit/debit cards accepted.

Experience the hair-raising Wolf Howl-In with our resident wolf expert. Pre-booking essential. For details & prices please phone: 01985 844328.

FREE ATTRACTIONS

- **A** Longleat House Scale Model
- **B** Family Bygones Exhibition
- **C** Needlecraft Centre
- **D** Life & Times of Henry, Lord Bath
- **E** Dolls House Emporium
- **F** Family State Coach

LONGLEAT ATTRACTIONS

- **1** Safari Park
- **2** Longleat House
- **3** Safari Boats
- **4** King Arthur's Mirror Maze
- **5** Doctor Who Exhibition
- **6** VirtuaScope Motion Ride
- **7** Pets Corner
- **8** Longleat Railway
- **9** Butterfly Garden
- **10** World's Longest Hedge Maze
- **11** Postman Pat Village
- **12** Adventure Castle

© Ballyhoo Publicity Ltd

Longleat

Geography learning objectives

◆ To express their own views about places and environments (1c).

◆ To use maps, plans and overhead views (2c).

◆ To identify and describe what places are like (3a).

◆ To identify where places are (3b).

◆ To make observations about where things are located and about other features in the environment (4a).

Vocabulary

Attraction, facilities, legend, key, family, wonderland, grounds, bird's-eye view, safari park, maze, labyrinth, opinion.

Discussing the text

◆ Look at the map together and read the title. Talk about similar maps or posters that the children have seen. Where did they see these? What did they say and what were they showing or advertising?

◆ Who has heard of Longleat or been there? Is it most famous for its safari park? Talk about visits the children have made to a place like this or pleasure parks like Barry Island or Alton Towers. Brainstorm words to describe these visits. Talk about sights, sounds and feelings.

◆ Read the title again and the boxed text, making sure the children understand the vocabulary. Help the children to notice the tone and what the text is trying to achieve – giving information but also advertising. Ask the children to pick out key words and phrases, such as *wonderland, attractions, range, much, much more!, hair-raising*, and to suggest alternatives that keep the lively tone.

◆ Look at the legends (keys). Make sure the children understand how to use them, looking for the relevant number and letter codes on the map. Do the attractions sound exciting? (You could contact the Estate Office on 01985 844400 for additional material.) Introduce the children to the idea of opinion and discuss how people who visit Longleat will think different things about their visits. Ask anyone who has visited if it was what they had expected. Which attractions did they go to? What animals did they see? Was the VirtuaScope ride fun? Did anyone have similar or different likes and dislikes about the place?

Geography activities

◆ Look at the map and ask the children to identify as many features of the park as they can. Check by using the keys. Look outside the main area of the park and point out the roads that come in from the north-west and west. Is the term *bird's-eye view* a good one to describe the illustration?

◆ Ask the children to find the Safari Park. Where is it? (It is far away from the rest of the park, enclosed by a fence, full of trees.) Why do they think it is there? Talk about the meaning of *Safari*. Does this word give any clue about what sort of animals might be kept in the park? (Dangerous ones and shy ones.) What sort of safety measures might be needed? Who needs protecting? (The people need protecting from the animals, but the animals also need to be protected from the people.) Can the children see the cars on the road that winds through the woods? Why do the children think the road bends so much? (So the people can see as much as possible and to keep them travelling slowly.)

GEOGRAPHICAL SKILLS

◆ The animals need protecting in another sense. Some of them are endangered species. Discuss how safari parks and zoos might be useful in protecting species (for example, by breeding new animals). How might they be a disadvantage to animals? (If there were lots of zoos and wildlife parks wanting to buy animals for show, then there would be a trade in animals taken from the wild and so there may not be enough left in the wild to breed a sustainable group.) Let the children research in groups different animals that are endangered and explain what a safari park could do for them.

◆ Ask the children to imagine they want to plan a route round Longleat after they have been to the safari park. Where will they start? (For example, at the house entrance or the car park.) What will they need to plan into their visit? (A stop for toilets, refreshments, something to eat.) What is the best weather for visiting? Are there plenty of things to do indoors if the weather is not good?

◆ Discuss how comprehensive the facilities are. Are there enough toilets? Are they in the right places? Perhaps challenge the children to think of something else that would be useful. Are there sufficient disabled toilets and in good positions, for example? If the children had the task of designing a new attraction, what would they put in? Where would be the best place to put it? What extra facilities for visitors would be needed if it is a big attraction?

◆ Ask the children to notice all the open areas and trees around the edge of the park. Does it seem quite a way from anywhere else, according to the poster? Would you be able to walk to it? Is it likely to be full of cars and coaches during the holidays? What are some of the problems a big park development such as Longleat might bring to places nearby? (Heavy traffic through local towns and villages, crowds of people.) What benefits do attractions like this bring? (Perhaps increased tourist spending in local towns, the educational, cultural and environmental value of supporting the house and wildlife park.)

◆ Discuss with the children what they have in the way of parks or amusement places in their own area. Ask them to draw a plan or picture to show what they would like to see in a small pleasure park near the school. Advise them that they will need to identify a site for their park. What will they need to think about? (Enough space, not too near houses, the noise that may be created, enough car parking and near to good road access.)

◆ Use a sand tray to create a pleasure park with good road access and lots of things to do. Remind the children to plan in the car parks and roads.

Further literacy ideas

◆ Look at *Dolls House Emporium*, for instance. Draw attention to the use of capital letters. Why are they used here? (For proper nouns.) Revise other examples where capital letters are used.

◆ Investigate characteristic pleasure park words, for example *family, attractions, refreshments, gift shop*. Ask the children to look at posters, brochures, similar maps and advertising material for other attractions. What words come up in most of the examples? Are there any common words that seem to be 'missing' from this text, such as *admission*?

◆ Look at 'hidden' words within words in the text, for example *Longleat, safari, information*. Extend this work by asking the children to look at other posters or in their reading books for similar words.

◆ Ask the children write a story set in the park. Perhaps set a scene, such as *You are driving round the safari park and you see an animal that is obviously ill…* Or it could be getting lost in a maze or meeting a ghost in the house. Ask the children to work in groups to think up some possible plots.

◆ Ask the children to design a poster to advertise Longleat. Tell them that you do not want it to show a map, but it could include, for example, illustrations of some of the animals. Advise them to pick out the most exciting attractions to include in their text. Remind them of the sort of persuasive language they have seen in this text and other posters.

Cops and Robbers

Genre
story
illustration
including a
labelled and
annotated
map

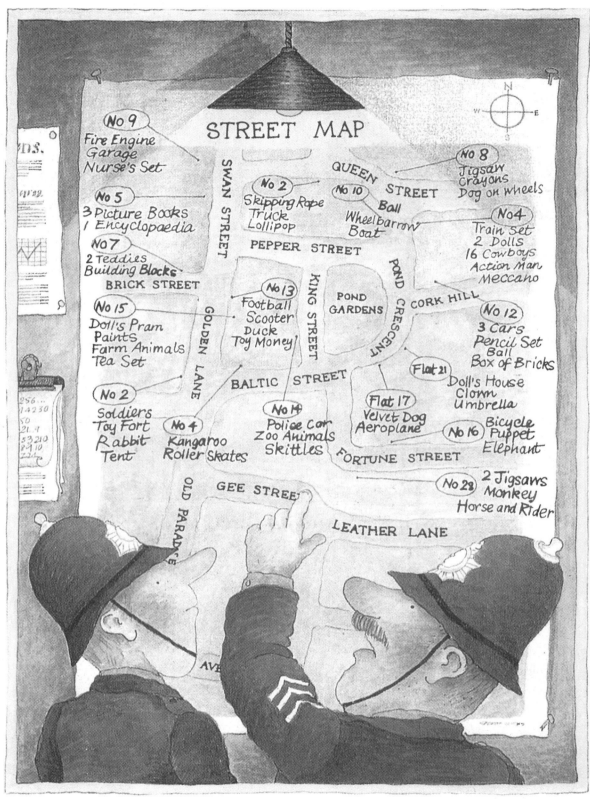

Janet and Allan Ahlberg

Cops and Robbers

Geography learning objectives

◆ To communicate in different ways (1d).

◆ To use geographical vocabulary in giving directions (2a).

◆ To use maps and plans (2c).

◆ To make maps and plans (2e).

◆ To identify and describe what places are like (3a).

Background notes

This extract uses a map on which additional information has been plotted, developing map literacy and enabling the children to practise retrieving information.

Vocabulary

Street lights, lane, road, corner, parade, crescent, compass, street furniture.

Discussing the text

◆ Get the children to look at the picture and tell you what it shows. (A street map on a wall, with policemen discussing it.) What has been marked on the map? Who has written the labels and lists? There are lots of numbers on the map. What do they refer to? (House numbers.) Why are these houses marked? (They are places where crimes have been committed).

◆ What are all the lists? (Items stolen and where they were stolen from – use the title, 'Cops and Robbers', as a clue.) When the children have identified what the map shows, discuss other possible reasons for having a map like this. It could be showing, for example, where people who bought particular items from a school fête live.

◆ Choose some words at random from the text and ask the children to read them aloud. Show them how to split the words into phonemes to aid reading and spelling the different words.

◆ Cover up some parts of the text, for example *Box of* ___, *Horse and* ___, and ask the children to predict what the missing words could be. Compare the children's suggestions with those actually written by the author.

◆ Make a list on the board of the street names on the map. Talk about how names of streets and places begin with capital letters. Write down the names of some of the streets where the children live. This could be used as the starting point for work on the children being familiar with and knowing how to write their own address. Talk about other common uses of capitalisation, such as in names for people, animals, books, television programmes, towns and countries.

◆ Ask the children to imagine that they are one of the people who has had some of the things listed on the map taken. Get them to role-play the conversations that would take place between these people and the police.

Geography activities

◆ Examine the layout of the street map. What does it show and what doesn't it show? (For example, actual houses.) How many different words can they find for a type of road? (*Lane, Parade, Hill, Street* and *Crescent.*) Can they think of any that are not included here? (For example, *Close, Path, Avenue.*)

◆ See if the children can find the compass at the top of the picture. Use a large classroom compass to demonstrate and remind the children of the main compass points. Then ask questions about the direction of places and streets on the map. For example, *In which direction from 12 Cork Hill is 13 Golden Lane?* This exercise can be developed in the school grounds. Stand outside with a compass and find which direction is north. If the children look that way, what can they see? The compass points can be marked onto the school playground. From which position is the best view all round?

◆ Discuss with the children what an average road looks like. What sort of houses will there be? Terraced, detached, semi-detached? What else might there be, for example, shops, public buildings, a car park, garage? What sort of street furniture will be there? (Perhaps street lights, benches, postbox, telephone box, bus stop.) Ask the children to describe the road they live in, listing as many of these features as they can remember.

◆ Ask the children to choose one of the streets on the map and draw a large picture of it, marking in the types of buildings and street furniture they might find there. If, as a class, they follow the correct lines of the street as shown on the map, they should be able to join up their pictures to mirror the map.

◆ Talk about giving street directions and try some examples using the street map. Increase the challenge by asking the children to follow multiple instructions in order to arrive at a given place. This can be repeated by using a street map of the local area or the local town, with instructions to find specific places. When the children feel confident to do this ask them to make up instructions for a partner. This can be developed into writing instructions to follow around the school or school grounds. Remind the children how to write instructions – in sequence; one at a time; using clear, directional language to avoid confusion.

◆ Encourage the children to make up a series of basic maps on a variety of themes, such as coming to school, going to visit a relative, or a shopping expedition. They can also map out a route from a journey in a story book.

Further literacy ideas

◆ Look at *Kangaroo*, one of the toys stolen from 4 Baltic Street. Ask the children to practise saying the word and go on to investigate other words that contain *oo*. Ask the children to make lists and, if they can, sentences of other *oo* words, for example *We saw a kangaroo in a zoo*.

◆ Ask the children to select a specified number of items from the map. For example *three* could be *jigsaw*, *puppet* and *train set*, and ask them to write sentences that include these items. More able children may be able to write 100-word stories that include these items.

◆ Go on a syllable hunt. Get the children to make a table with columns for words with one, two or three syllables. Ask them to find words on the map for each column.

◆ Look for words within words in the text. Ask the children to write down all the words that are made up of two smaller words joined together, for example *jigsaw*, *football*, *wheelbarrow*. Then ask them to find other examples of compound words in their reading books and add them to their list.

◆ Use the information on the map as the basis for writing simple sentences about the story. For example, *Some soldiers were taken from the house at 2 Golden Lane*. More able children could be encouraged to include more than one item and separate them by commas, for example …*some soldiers, a toy fort, a rabbit and a tent were taken*.

◆ Ask the children to find all the words on the map that contain double consonants, such as *puppets, teddies, rabbit*. Ask the children to add to this list using their reading books.

◆ Ask the children to write their own story set in the streets shown on the map. Encourage them to include as many of the different places as they can.

Going to the country – part 1

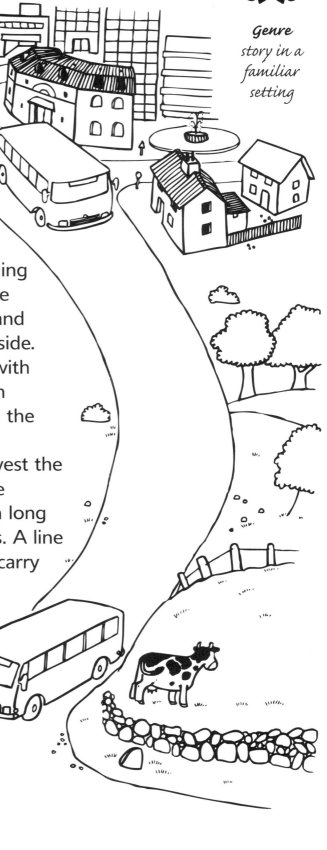

Genre
story in a
familiar
setting

Waiting at the city bus stop were Sanjay and his friend Anna. Sanjay's Uncle Saeed was taking them for a ride into the country to a very pretty village where he promised they would have really, really BIG ice creams!

Sitting on the top deck of the bus, they had a wonderful view. They passed through the busy city centre with its bustling crowds out shopping, then on through the quiet suburbs with the strings of houses and corner shops, and at last into the countryside.

The road became narrower and fields with hedges bordered each side. As it was high summer, the wheat stalks gently shook in the breeze.

Uncle said, "It will soon be time to harvest the wheat, using big machines called combine harvesters." They passed small farms with long drives and houses standing by themselves. A line of pylons snaked across the fields. "They carry electricity," said Uncle Saeed.

The bus climbed a long hill. As it reached the top, everyone could see the village in front of them. In the centre, the church spire stood out above the houses.

"Hurray, we're here!" said Sanjay when they arrived.

"Let's go and explore!" said Anna.

Paula Richardson

Going to the country – part 1

Geography learning objectives

◆ To use geographical vocabulary (2a).

◆ To make maps and plans (2e).

◆ To identify human activities and jobs in both town and country (3a).

◆ To recognise and compare rural and urban features (3a, 3d, 4a).

Background notes

This text, with the one that follows, forms a short story about a visit to a village. The journey from city to village is described, drawing attention to the importance of farming to the rural landscape and economy. The second part looks at the village itself.

Vocabulary

City, town, suburb, village, country, shop, farm, pylon, church, spire, wheat, harvest.

Discussing the text

◆ Show the children the passage and read it through, up to *they had a wonderful view*. Ask the children to predict what the characters in the story saw on their journey. A list of these could be made and then compared with those things actually described in the text.

◆ Read the rest of the text through with the children and ask them if they have ever been on a journey like the one described – going from a town to the countryside or vice versa. Talk about the trip, when it was and what they saw along the way. Do they remember who they were with and why they made the journey?

◆ Re-read the text and highlight all the words or sentences that give information about the settings for this story, for example *busy city centre*. Go through unfamiliar vocabulary, such as *quiet suburbs*.

◆ Do the children notice that this is only the first part of the story? Ask them to predict what part 2 might be about.

◆ Through shared reading, you could model how to retell the story so far in their own words. Discuss with the children what elements of the story stayed the same in the retelling (the essential facts) and what elements changed (for example, the vocabulary).

◆ When reading the story with or to the children, have some words covered up and ask the children to read on and back, using contextual clues to work out what words might be used. Discuss the children's suggestions. Do they differ from the author's? Do they work as well as those in the original? Are they better, even?

Geography activities

◆ Talk about where the children in the story live. Is it in the countryside or in a town or city? Do they live in the centre? (No, they *passed through* the city centre.) Perhaps they live in the suburbs or on an estate near the centre. What do we mean by *suburb*? Discuss this with the children and identify some local examples.

◆ With the children's help, sequence the story using geographical features as waypoints and write these in order down the left-hand side of a flip chart. Ask the children to identify what activities or work goes on in each area, looking for clues in the text. Fill in the details next to each waypoint. Ask the children for other details, such as *busy*, *narrow roads*, *hedges*, *fields*.

◆ Focus on the reference to electricity pylons. Can the children describe a pylon? How many similar features can the children think of? (Telephone poles, electricity poles, radio and television masts, telephone masts and so on.) Why are they needed? How would life be different without them?

◆ Remind the class that the children in the story have come to a village from a city. How are they different? Divide a flip chart page in two and brainstorm the differences, listing them on the chart. Ask the children to try to match each idea in one column with a contrasting one in the other. Then ask them to write descriptive sentences about each place, bringing out the contrasting features.

◆ The story mentions wheat and harvest. Let the children find out more about the farming of wheat. Advise them to look at when it is sown and harvested, what preparation of fields is done and so on. Ask them to draw up a flow chart to show the production of wheat, then think of what other crops the children might see on a trip through the countryside.

◆ Ask the children to make a simple map of the route. Tell them to add labels to identify the various features mentioned in the story. This is a good opportunity to introduce some simple map symbols, for example a church with a spire, a bus station, pylons.

Further literacy ideas

◆ Ask the children to make a flow chart of the journey, showing the different features passed in the right order. Tell them to add notes on how these features appear in the story, for example *busy city centre – bustling crowds shopping*.

◆ There are many interesting descriptive words in the passage. Take this opportunity to revise work on adjectives. Stress the term *adjective* and then, in a guided reading session, ask the children to highlight the adjectives in the text. An extension activity could involve the children coming up with alternative adjectives that could be used without altering the meaning of the passage.

◆ Ask the children to use the country setting to write a short story with the same characters. Their story could begin with the closing sentence of this one – *'Let's go and explore!' said Anna*. Alternatively, the children could write their own story loosely based on this text. Have they ever been on a journey with a friend or relative to somewhere new and exciting? Advise the children that they should describe the setting in clear detail to make it vivid for the reader, as this author has done.

◆ Point out that, by contrast, the text says very little about the characters in the story. Ask the children to rewrite all or part of the story, adding details that will tell the reader more about the characters. It may help to start by writing a profile for the character chosen and then thinking about how such a character might behave or what they would do in the situation described in the story.

◆ Ask the children to summarise the story so far. It may be helpful to limit the number of words they are allowed to 30 or 50, depending on ability.

◆ In a guided reading session, ask the children to highlight the speech. Then let them make a simple picture book of the story, or a comic strip, with the spoken words in speech bubbles.

◆ Ask the children to think about how a setting influences a story and ask them to try to write a similar story based in a different setting. Perhaps Uncle Saeed takes the children on a trip to a wildlife park or a theme park. Tell the children to describe the place and what the characters do there.

Going to the country – part 2

Genre
story in a
familiar
setting

"Which way shall we go?" asked Sanjay.

"I think this road leads into the village and perhaps to the ice cream shop," replied his uncle. "First we must check the timetable at the bus stop."

"Why?" asked Anna.

"Because buses don't run very often in the country," laughed Uncle, "and we don't want to be left here until tomorrow!"

They walked up the road, past some rows of terraced houses on the left and some semi-detached houses on the right. At the end of the road, they turned a corner and saw the village green with a duck pond in the middle. "Oh!" gasped Anna. "Isn't it pretty?"

Across the green was the church with the spire and next to it was the village hall. Around the green were some old cottages and a pub with a sign that said, 'The Cricket Bat'. Next to the pub was a small shop with a big ice cream sign by the door.

"Hurray!" shouted Sanjay and Anna when they saw it. They all sat on the benches beside the pond to eat their really big ice creams. "I'm going to give the last bit of my cornet to the ducks," said Anna.

"What a lovely day out," they all agreed.

Paula Richardson

Going to the country – part 2

Geography learning objectives

◆ To make a simple maps (2e).

◆ To identify and describe common features of villages (3a).

◆ To compare some features of urban and rural life (3d).

Vocabulary

Village, shop, timetable, terraced, semi-detached, cottage, village green, pond, pub.

Discussing the text

◆ Read the text through a couple of times, with the children taking it in turns to play the parts of the characters. Talk about reading with expression. How do the children think Anna and Sanjay would have said *Hurray!* at the end of the story. Would they have been excited and pleased or sad and bored? Get the children to role-play the characters, speaking in different tones of voice. Ask them to notice how this affects the story.

◆ Ask the children to recall what happened in part 1 of the story. How much of the description of the journey can they remember? Re-read part 2 and decide how it is similar to or different from what the children expected to happen. Did the children enjoy the story? Can they think of anything that they could add to the story to make it more interesting and exciting (but still realistic!)?

◆ Are there any clues in the passage about the weather or time of year that the story is set in? Ask the children to suggest words and phrases that could be added to the text to give more information about these things.

Geography activities

◆ Focus on some of the details of the village. Is this a small one or a large one? (The indications are that it is quite small.) How might a large village be different? (The larger a village grows, the more it becomes like a town – better bus services, more shops and facilities.)

◆ What is the big difference between the city where Sanjay and Anna live and the village they are visiting, as far as buses are concerned? Discuss *why* the bus service to a small village is likely to be more infrequent than in a large town or city.

◆ This second part of the story lends itself more to drawing a map of a small *area*, rather than a linear route map, as in part 1. Start by talking about the village green. What do we know about it? List on a flip chart everything we can tell. (For example, the church and village hall are across the green from the road; it has a pond; there are some cottages, a pub and a shop around it.) Anything else? Can we guess at other features, such as another road? Ask the children to make a map of the village and its green. What do we know about the road leading to the green? Is it straight? What buildings are along it?

◆ Ask the children what the family would have had to do if they had missed the bus. Could they have stayed overnight? Where, perhaps? If not, could they have got a taxi? How? Where would it have had to come from? In groups, get the children to produce a six-illustration story, with text either added underneath or in speech bubbles, entitled 'Missing the bus'.

◆ As far as we know, the village has one shop. Talk about what the shop is likely to sell. Might it also be a post office? Do the children think there might be other shops, for example a mobile shop, perhaps even a mobile library? Discuss why these are so useful. Where would people from the village go to do their main shopping? How would they get there? Would they use the infrequent bus service or are they more likely to use their cars? Children can make a list of all the facilities and services they would need, starting with those above. Against each item, they could explain where they think the village residents would have to go for it.

◆ How might the village be different in winter? Discuss the problems that snow can cause out in open countryside and remote villages. Talk about why the problems are more severe in the countryside than in the middle of a town or city. The Postman Pat story *Letters on Ice* by John Cunliffe (Scholastic: Hippo) illustrates some of these issues, as well as bringing out other aspects of village life. It could be used in an extension to this work. Get the children to write descriptions of 'The village in summer' and 'The village in winter'. Emphasise that they need to use language that will be descriptive and create atmosphere.

Further literacy ideas

◆ Role-play the story in small groups. The children could try to add their own actions to the dialogue and then perform it to the rest of the class.

◆ Ask the children a series of comprehension questions about the text, for example *What did the children pass on their way to the village green?* Remind the children that their answers need to be written in full sentences with capital letters and full stops.

◆ Examine the punctuation used. Do the children notice all the exclamation marks? What about punctuation of dialogue? How is speech indicated? Ask the children to circle the speech marks and highlight the words that are spoken. Help the children to see how the speech marks go around the spoken words.

◆ Write out some sentences from the text and ask the children to change them into either the present or future tense. For example *Across the green was the church with the spire* would become *Across the green is the church with the spire* in the present tense.

◆ Make a list of all the words for *said* used in the two parts of the story, and put it up for children to refer to when writing. Get the children to suggest more that could be used. This can be extended to other actions, for example *walk*, *run*, *stamp*, *creep*,

◆ Similarly, use the descriptions *lovely day out* and *really big ice creams* as a basis for encouraging the children to use variety and vivid description in their writing. Can they think of alternative words for these descriptions, perhaps *enormous ice creams*?

◆ Ask the children to add a character to the story, using the setting for ideas. They could include, for instance, the shopkeeper. In a guided writing session, decide on a character to add and write a profile. Help the children to rewrite the story with this new character. Emphasise the need for the character to be described in enough detail for the reader to be able to picture him or her and that he or she should be involved in the action of the story in some way.

◆ Ask the children to imagine what happens next in the story and to write a description of the journey home. What happens if the bus is late? What do the characters plan to do?

◆ Reproduce this part of the story with some deliberate spelling and/or punctuation errors. Ask the children to highlight the mistakes or write out the passage correctly, according to ability.

◆ Ask the children to write a poem entitled 'The Really Big Ice Cream'. Encourage them to write about their feelings by saying, for example *Think about how you feel as you wait to buy it. How does it taste when you start to eat it?* See if they can write their poems in the shape of an ice cream cone.

Using an atlas

Genre
contents and index pages of an atlas

Contents

Index

Using an atlas

Geography learning objectives

◆ To use geographical vocabulary (2a).

◆ To use maps and plans (2c).

◆ To recognise how places are linked to other places in the world (3e).

◆ To identify and describe where places are (3b).

Background notes

The use of an atlas is essential in geography, both to find out specific information and to develop world awareness. As with all reference books, knowing how and when to use the contents and index is an essential skill. This text will lead into further work with whatever atlases you have available in your school.

Vocabulary

Atlas, map, world, physical, human, Europe, America, Africa, Australia, polar, space, ocean, index, continent, country, city.

Discussing the text

◆ Focus on the headings *Contents* and *Index*. What is each of these things and where do we find them? In which parts of a book do you find them? Look at other examples of contents and index pages with the children. Can they identify any similarities or differences between them? What are they both doing for the reader?

◆ Look at the arrangement of each list. Why is the index page written in alphabetical order? Could the contents be written in alphabetical order? Why do the children think it is written as it is?

◆ Talk about what an atlas is. What sort of book is it – fiction or non-fiction? Have the children used atlases before? Why would people look in an atlas? What sort of information do we find in atlases?

◆ Look more closely at the contents vocabulary. Can the children guess what *polar* means? What do the numbers on the contents page refer to? What would happen if they were not included?

◆ Move on to some examples from the index. What does UK stand for? Why is it written like this? Where have the children seen other similar abbreviations? Go on to look at the abbreviations for mountain and mountains to make sure the children understand them.

◆ Check that the children understand the purpose of both the contents and index and how they work by asking them questions like *On what page would you find a map of Australia?*

◆ Discuss the numbers and letters in brackets in the index. Do any of the children know why they are there? They may be able to recall work that they have done in numeracy to help them with these grid references.

Geography activities

◆ Discuss how to find a particular place in an atlas. Illustrate this by using some examples of other atlases to show how the references on the contents, maps and index pages fit together. Using the atlases, demonstrate to the children how the pages in this text would come at the beginning and end of an atlas. What does the text not show? (The maps.)

◆ Focus on the contents page. Which country has the most information about it? Why do the children think this might be? Do they know which areas will be covered by *Polar regions*? What will the information on page 12 be about? How might this information have been collected? Show some photographs taken from space so the children can see the shape of the land masses. What is not so easily seen from space?

◆ Examine the index page. Ask the children about the information they will find on specific pages. Why is *Cambridge* included twice? (You could explain that this is similar to a class where two children with the same name might be called Emma C and Emma P.) Ask the children to sort the examples on this page into physical and human features. Which one does not fit so well into these categories?

◆ Demonstrate how to use an atlas. Practise finding some places with everyone together, and help the children to work out whether using the contents page or the index is most helpful. (Explain that it could depend on how much information or knowledge the user has already.) With the children working in pairs or in small groups, give them a list of countries to find. Tell them they have to identify the pages they are on and their positions on the page.

This activity can be made more challenging by asking the children to find cities as well as countries. Draw up a chart that has headings such as *Continent*, *Country* and *City* for the children to fill in as they find the answers, perhaps something like this:

Continent	Country	City
Africa		Cairo
South America	Equador	

◆ Discuss with the class the idea of using a country or continent outline to write a poem in or to fill with pictures which represent the place. How will they research the information they need?

◆ Provide a number of pictures representing scenes and climatic zones around the world. Talk about the characteristics of these and ask the children in pairs to find some reference books and atlases to help them identify countries where these might be found. This exercise is most suitable for more able children to complete, but with support, it can be done with children of a range of abilities.

Further literacy ideas

◆ Give the children part of or all of the index cut into pieces, and ask them to sort it into alphabetical order without referring to the original text. Include some words that are not used in the original text to extend this work. This could lead to or on from work on dictionary skills and how it is sometimes necessary to look at the second and even third letter of a word in order to place it correctly.

◆ Let the children choose one place from the index page and use reference books to find out a few interesting facts. These could be written up either as a series of sentences or as a fluent paragraph, according to the ability of the children.

◆ Prepare a series of questions based on understanding of how the information is ordered. For example, *Does the map of South America come before or after the map of the Polar Regions?*

◆ Use the text as a starting point for work on proper nouns. How can the children tell something is a proper noun? Ask them to look at one or two of their reading books and to write down all the proper nouns that they can find. Then ask them to pick out which of those are names of places.

◆ Ask the children to imagine you are going to write a book on a current class topic and it needs a contents page and an index page. This may work best as a shared writing lesson, with all the children brainstorming ideas of suitable subjects for the contents and index before you demonstrate sorting and ordering the information. For example, an index on transport could include entries on cars, buses, railway lines, trams, airports and so on.

Geographical dictionary

Genre
explanation
– illustrated
dictionary
definitions

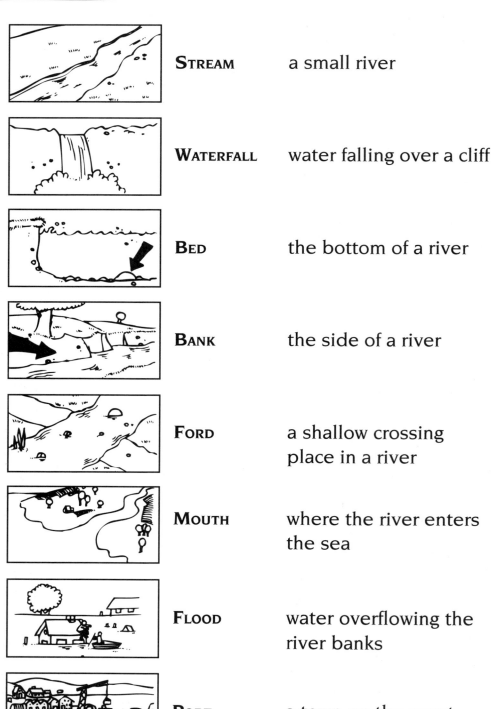

	STREAM	a small river
	WATERFALL	water falling over a cliff
	BED	the bottom of a river
	BANK	the side of a river
	FORD	a shallow crossing place in a river
	MOUTH	where the river enters the sea
	FLOOD	water overflowing the river banks
	PORT	a town on the coast where ships dock
	BRIDGE	a crossing over a river

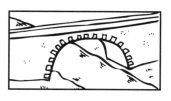

Geographical dictionary

Geography learning objectives

◆ To use geographical vocabulary (2a).

◆ To use maps and plans (2c).

◆ To make maps and plans (2e).

◆ To identify and describe what rivers are like (3a).

◆ To recognise changes in physical and human features (4b).

Vocabulary

Stream, waterfall, bed, bank, ford, mouth, flood, port, bridge, coast, cliff, reservoir, well.

Discussing the text

◆ Look at the heading with the children and discuss the word *dictionary*. What is a dictionary and what is it used for? Use this discussion as a starting point for looking at a variety of dictionaries. Include those with illustrations and those without. Ask the children to think of examples of other subject dictionaries, such as musical and mathematical. Talk about the differences between a general dictionary and a dictionary specific to one subject. Do subject dictionaries go into more detail? Do they include words not in a general dictionary? If possible, show the children a selection of subject-based dictionaries. Then talk about *geographical*. Talk about what geography is and explain how the word *geographical* comes from the word *geography*. Discuss other words like this, such as *history – historical* and compare the text to, for instance, the musical and mathematical dictionaries you have just looked at.

◆ Read through the headwords and look at the way they are set out. Do the children think they would be set out in this order in a normal dictionary? Bring in the term *alphabetical* at this point and make sure the children understand it. Orally reorder the words and discuss what happens when the first letter of two words is the same. Show the children how to look at the second and even the third letters of the words.

◆ Read through each of the terms with the children. Discuss any of the features that the children have seen. Where were they when they saw them? Do the children notice that all the features relate to water and specifically to rivers? Discuss the purpose of the diagrams. Are they helpful to understanding?

◆ Look at any of the words that have more than one meaning, for example *mouth* and *bank*. Talk about how these would be shown in a general dictionary. For example, *mouth (1)* and *mouth (2)*, with the relevant definition for each.

Geography activities

◆ Discuss each of the features that the dictionary is defining. Show pictures of a river and ask the children to identify the features in the word list. Why would a waterfall be in the early stages of the river? Why would a port be at the coast? Make a display of river pictures and ask the children to make labels for the main river features.

◆ Photocopy and cut up the words and descriptions and ask the children to place them in the correct location on a big floor map or a river drawn out on a large piece of paper. Is there sometimes a choice of places for the labels? Invite discussion as to where they could be correctly positioned. What other things might be found near a river? Ask the children to put in farms, animals, villages and a port using model houses and other model features.

◆ Help the children to apply this model of a geographical dictionary to another set of features such as the coast or a mountain. Ask the children to compile a list of words to do with the coast – *waves*, *beach*, *cliffs*, *rock pools*, *sand*, *sea* and so on. You could then do the same kind of exercises as you did with river features. Pictures of a variety of coastal features will aid the thinking on vocabulary work.

◆ Photocopy and then cut up the various words, definitions, and pictures to create a variety of games, such as 'Mix and match', 'Snap' and 'Three in a row'. Encourage the children to create some of their own games with the cards.

◆ Make a wall collage to show different types of physical environment, such as a mountain. Ask the children to make labels for all the features, on which they should include a simple definition.

◆ Talk to the children about an aspect of rivers, such as flooding. Why does this happen? When? How will it affect the land round the river? Show pictures, video clips or news items of floods. What is happening? How does it affect people? Ask the children to imagine that they have had a flood warning to leave their homes quickly. Where would they go and which three possessions would they choose to take with them?

◆ On a map of the UK, mark some rivers and ask the children to work in pairs to name them with the help of an atlas. Some children will be able to name rivers in other countries.

◆ Use an OS map to show the children where and how rivers are marked. All water features are marked in blue and so are very easy to see. Ask them to find features such as different parts of a river as well as lakes, coastlines or wells. Discuss what a reservoir is and explain that they often have straight sides that indicate they are part of the built environment.

Further literacy ideas

◆ Ask the children to sort the words shown in the text into alphabetical order. This work can be extended by including additional words that have the same first and even second letters.

◆ Give the children a list of words related to those in the text, and ask them to use dictionaries to find definitions for them.

◆ Separate and mix up the headwords and their definitions, and ask the children to match each word with its definition. This exercise could be completed for any set of words and more able children could even use a dictionary to create their own exercise for their work partners.

◆ Ask the children to find and record alternative definitions for the words *bank* and *mouth*. Then encourage them to find other homographs – words that are spelled the same but have more than one meaning.

◆ Challenge the children to write a short story or poem that includes as many of the headwords from the list as possible. You could specify the maximum number of words their story or poem can contain.

◆ Give the children a comprehension-type cloze procedure based on the text, for example *The place where a river ____ the sea is called the mouth.*

◆ Use the text as a starting point for exploring rhyming words like *flood* and *mud*. Challenge the children to come up with as many words as they can to rhyme with the starting words. Examine how the letter patterns in some of these words are similar and how some are different.

◆ Use words from the text to investigate and practise spelling of initial consonant blends, such as <u>str</u>eam – <u>str</u>ing, <u>str</u>ong; <u>fl</u>ood – <u>fl</u>ight.

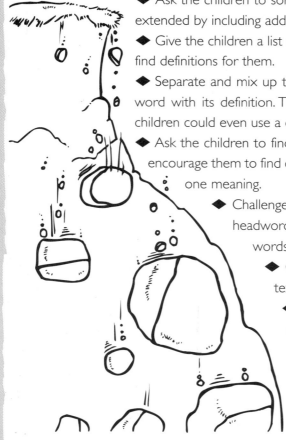